TEA POT 4 PLEASURE (handwritten inscription)

HOUSING AND THE CITY

LOVE *versus* HOPE

by Daniel Solomon

Schiffer Publishing Ltd®

4880 Lower Valley Road • Atglen, PA 19310

Other Schiffer Books on Related Subjects:

Anatomy of a Great Home, Boyce Thompson, ISBN 978-0-7643-5465-6

Small Dreams, Jeffrey Milstein, ISBN 978-0-7643-5247-8

Designed by Kristen Bakken
Cover design by Kristen Bakken
Cover photo: Fred Lyon
Cosponsored by the Centre for the Future of Places,
Royal Institute of Technology, Stockholm

Type set in Minion Pro

ISBN: 978-0-7643-5643-8

Printed in China

Published by Schiffer Publishing, Ltd.
4880 Lower Valley Road
Atglen, PA 19310
Phone: (610) 593-1777; Fax: (610) 593-2002
E-mail: Info@schifferbooks.com
Web: www.schifferbooks.com

For our complete selection of fine books on this and related subjects, please visit our website at www.schifferbooks.com. You may also write for a free catalog.

Schiffer Publishing's titles are available at special discounts for bulk purchases for sales promotions or premiums. Special editions, including personalized covers, corporate imprints, and excerpts, can be created in large quantities for special needs. For more information, contact the publisher.

We are always looking for people to write books on new and related subjects. If you have an idea for a book, please contact us at proposals@schifferbooks.com.

Contents

The 1989 Loma Prieta earthquake destroyed San Francisco's Central Freeway, which had ruptured the city thirty years earlier. Since then, new development shown in red has repaired and brought new life to the center of the city.

From the Market Octavia plan; San Francisco Department of City Planning and Daniel Solomon Design Partners

PART I: THE CONTINUOUS CITY AND THE RUPTURED CITY

A Historical Memoir

Central Freeway, San Francisco, 1959

". . . if my censors be not satisfied with the common verdict of opinion, let them rest content with that of time, which in the end reveals the hidden defects of everything, and being father of truth and judge without passion, ever passes on men's writings just sentence of life or death."[1]

—BALDASSARE CASTIGLIONE

CHAPTER 1

Love versus Hope: Ameliorating Force or Wedge?

Autobiography Meets History

The author has spent the last half century as an architect and as a teacher, an increasingly rare pairing of occupations. This double life has combined many features of a blessing with some significant traits of a curse. The blessing part includes the incredible euphoric rush of seeing one's imaginings realized as buildings—real places where people live, work, and breed. The euphoric rush is multiplied if you can sometimes build places of beauty and dignity for people who have been denied such things before. If one is susceptible to this form of intoxication, there is really nothing like it.

The hard part of combining the roles of working architect and pedagogue—the curse—is the gnawing compulsion to make sense of what one is doing, as opposed to merely doing it and finding pleasure in the doing. One has only to look at the world as it been built in recent times to realize that making sense of what one does is not an altogether common practice for architects. So much makes so little sense to so many.

This book is my attempt at sense-making—a coming to terms with history, for me and for my contemporaries. This history did not begin anew when I became an architect; the circumstances in which I have worked were well formed by tumultuous events and giant personalities in the half century before my half century. Looking beyond the strewn battlefield of my own endeavors, I see it as part of a great century of conflict—unresolved conflict that continues to surround everyone engaged in the building of cities or parts of them, especially the parts where people live.

This is not an autobiography or an architectural monograph; it is not a history book, nor is it just random musings. It has elements of all of these genres, linked together by the chain of an idea. It is a reflection on the urban upheavals that occurred immediately prior to and during my years as an architect and urbanist. I put this forth as a proposition about architecture and town planning's potential for social good or unintended harm, and as observations about some urban triumphs and some massive urban disasters.

Despite its strange absence from political discourse, housing is a matter of great urgency. All around the world, in the cities that drive technological change and the formation of staggering wealth, there is fierce struggle over housing stock between long-established communities and the perpetrators and beneficiaries of a new economy. Some of the most explosively prosperous American cities are overrun with the grotesque tragedy of intractable homelessness. At a much larger scale, all the world shudders or simply averts its eyes from the plight of sixty-five million refugees. Religious and political strife and the ravages of climate change will continue. The displacement of tens of millions of people from one cultural setting to another is a grim fact of the twenty-first century. Inadequate or wrong-headed response to housing those in need has been the catalyst for violence, which in turn hardens inaction's resolve. We are in a mess, and those of us who have struggled for decades against many obstacles to build decent accommodation for all sorts of people have some things to say on the matter.

The Ruptured City and the Continuous City

A powerful thread in the last century of urban history is the idea that the traditional city has been an impediment to a just, healthy, and egalitarian society. Much of the canon of modern architecture and urbanism evolved to dissociate a rational and scientific new order from the insalubrious disorder of the urban legacy. Almost a century of building worldwide has been directly shaped or profoundly influenced by this idea. However, the utopian future that once shone so brightly has now become a deeply flawed, sometimes tragic past. The twentieth-century story of modernist urbanism fueling the latent divisions of society and creating communities of fury and despair has chapters in many places, including my city, San Francisco. Architecture and urbanism cannot be neutral in these matters. For good or ill, by intent or happenstance, the architect is a social actor and has been for a long time. The hegemony of modernist urbanism is a project that was never quite completed. Here and there, for different reasons and at different times, the premodern city reshaped and reasserted itself robustly in response to modern circumstances. These were not revivalist movements; they were seamless adaptations of the built legacy of previous generations to radically new conditions. San Francisco is such a place, and San Francisco's reclamation of its own genius loci has been the context of much of my own work.

The principal creation myth of modernism in all its forms and incarnations is revolution. For a century, the most powerful of conventions has been the shattering of convention. Across a broad range of disciplines, upheaval is routine, expected, and demanded; acceptability is unacceptable; heterodoxy is orthodoxy.

There is nothing wrong with a state of perpetual revolution in the arts. It may be unfortunate that old skills and sensibilities atrophy as new ones evolve, but it is impossible to argue that the inventive, the critical, or the restlessly probing are linked to bad music, bad fiction, or bad painting. Perpetual revolution in these arts is healthy—as wit sharpening, as the builder of consciousness, as a political and social gyroscopic. Constant discontinuities between the present and the most recent past can serve cognitive growth. The best artists teach us new realities all the time and make us smarter; that is what they are for.

Modern urbanism and architecture also share the creation myth of perpetual iconoclasm—*the lure of heresy* [2]—in Peter Gay's memorable phrase. But urbanism and urban architecture reside in an entirely different category of endeavor from other arts. Urbanism and urban architecture, like the utensils of daily life, have no proscenium, no frame, and no decontextualizing white gallery wall. They are frameless, unbounded. They are not commentary on the life of the world; they *are* the life of the world. This absence of frame or proscenium is a crucial difference, a difference that frequently has turned the iconoclasm of modernism from healthy cognitive renewal into a toxic, self-devouring malignancy.

Discontinuity between present and past serves the arts well and the city badly. Relying on the theory of one to produce the reality of the other is a malign confusion. The tales told here are about architecture, urbanism, and the ruptures in society—architecture and urbanism as an ameliorating force, or architecture and urbanism as a hot wedge driven into a wound.

Social tensions always exist.

As this is written, the relationship of France to its Muslim minority and how they have been housed has been headline news for two decades. For earlier generations, the decanting of Italy's

Public housing, Paris

impoverished rural hinterlands into cities of modern industry and into the administrative heart of a new nation caused similar tensions. The high drama of Paris's and Rome's sharply different approaches to this issue is a textbook for these matters. It is a textbook for what should be a required course as sixty-five million desperate refugees from the Middle East, Africa, and South Asia scratch at the doors of the West.

In today's San Francisco, a young generation awash in the sudden and sometimes staggering wealth formation of the tech economy regularly confronts the tragedies and dangers—real and imaginary—posed by the homeless, drug gangs, and the dispossessed.

This book is the story of collision between two recurrent and mutually antagonistic dreams about cities, dreams that architects have cherished. A big part of each of these dreams has to do with how cities house or want to house their working people, their poor, and their newcomers. Both dreams have recurred in many countries over a period of at least ninety years. Both appeared before the emergence of fascism in Europe, persisted through it, and have carried on since. There has been ebb and flow between both dreams in the US since the 1930s. Both dreams have shaped parts of San Francisco as they shaped parts of Paris, Rome, Amsterdam, Stockholm, and New York.

These two quite opposite concepts of urbanity can be roughly equated with Love and with Hope, two highly touted human emotions, which, as every adult knows, have many really foolish manifestations. The clouded judgments that emanate from love and from hope constitute much of the world's literature, but writers on city planning don't normally deal with these subjects.

I will associate the city based on love with the term *the Continuous City*.

Let us then call the city founded on hope *the Ruptured City*.

Simply put: Love of the city and its layered history underpins the Continuous City. The Ruptured City has many sources, but first among them is the hope and belief that we can produce a city that is healthier, more rational, and more humane, especially for disadvantaged people, than the accreted layers of mess that urban history bequeathed. Hope is embedded so deeply in the proponents of the Ruptured City that they have been willing, even eager, destroyers of the urbanity they have seen as impediments to their vision.

Hope takes many forms and has many nuances of meaning. I must ask you, my readers, for the time you spend with this text, to accept use of the word for just those forms of hope that contain within them optimism—naive optimism—that by acting in a certain way we can ensure that conditions in the future will be fundamentally better than the present or the past, neither of which has been very good. This form of hope contains both hubris and contempt, and those who possess it claim previously unattained wisdom.

Sign by public housing tenants denoting their origins; Othello Station Seattle, project by Daniel Solomon Design Partners

The differences between the Continuous City and the Ruptured City are fundamental and easy to see. The Continuous City, or City of Love, is continuous in three ways, all intertwined. First, it is spatially continuous, or mostly so. Buildings join with one another to form a great continuum of built fabric—defining streets, lanes, squares, lanes, and courtyards. It is not full of holes and gaps, and freestanding buildings asserting their autonomous thinghood with space all around them are a rarity. Second, the Continuous City is temporally continuous. Past and present blend together, and the past is present in daily life, giving it depth and dimension like underpainting on canvas. In Aldo Rossi's beautiful words, a Continuous City is a "great encampment of the living and the dead."[3]

Finally, perhaps most importantly, the Continuous City is continuous socially. Everybody lives there; no one is excluded. It is the best place, really the only place, to experience the full range of human possibility close-up. If a Wall Street Master-of-the-Universe who lives uptown doesn't want to get stuck in traffic on the way to the office, he hops on the Lexington Avenue Express. For long minutes he can't help looking into the eyes of a thuggish sixteen-year-old and a Puerto Rican mom with two kids. He learns something about people whose life experience he cannot imagine. That happens on the Lexington Avenue Express all the time.

The typical Ruptured Cities of the late twentieth and twenty-first centuries have none of these properties. Think of places such as Tyson's Corner, Virginia, outside Washington, DC; virtually all of Orange County, California; much of Atlanta, Houston and Phoenix; and of the Paris Peripherique. In these places, buildings and streets each march to their own drummer (the architect and the traffic engineer, respectively), and they scarcely greet each other in passing. The result is a proliferation of holes and gaps, leftover fragments, and parking lots—a fractured townscape where it is unpleasant or pointless to walk anywhere.

The Ruptured City also tends to be perpetually new. Almost nothing is built to last very long and it doesn't. There is no patina of time and no presence of ancestors, no deep roots for anyone. The darkest and most destructive side of the Ruptured City is the segregation it tends to impose by race and class, the way in which many people's common life experience is restricted to their own kind.

An urban traveler with an eye for such things will discover that love (the Continuous City) has a far better track record when it comes to city building than hope (the Ruptured City), especially with regard to housing the needy. Hope's record, in fact, is so terrible in this regard that what has passed for hope for so long might be recast as hopeless; at least that is my hope in writing this book. It seems likely that at some point, the urgency of housing need will actually spur a response, and society will once more devote serious resources to providing housing for more than just the affluent. When that great day comes, it will be crucial to have clearly in focus what went right and what went horribly wrong in the sporadic but earnest attempts over the last century to house everyone decently.

The City of Hope has two sides: a front and a back that almost always look quite different from one another. We see the front of the City of Hope when it lies in the future, when its formulation is new and untested. We see the City of Hope from the back when it has been built for a while, when people have lived in it and it has been through the hot crucible of reality. Architects, particularly those with ties to academia, usually build their careers on the front view of Hope. On our journey we will look at a series of largely unexamined back views.

Just to make this difference between the front and the back of hope perfectly clear, let's look briefly at one example. In the 1930 master plan for Rome, Mussolini's chief planners and architects, Gustavo Giovannoni and Marcello Piacentini, looked forward with dreamy-eyed anticipation to the day when Rome's streets and broad new boulevards would swarm with automobile traffic, which they equated to the lifeblood of a living organism. Giovannoni and Piacentini were gifted and cultured men, and they were supported in this view by the governor of Rome, the most important Roman senators, and Mussolini himself. As everyone now knows, swarms of automobile traffic did not work out so well in Rome. In 2010 its entire historic center was declared a *zono pedonale*, off-limits to cars except by special permit.

In many places, the protagonists of both the Continuous City and the Ruptured City have articulated their case, sometimes poetically, and built large sections of city. On our journey from prologue to back cover, we will visit some places where the casting of good guys and bad guys is complex and ambiguous, but in the end, there is no possibility (as with traffic in central Rome) of getting mixed up about who was right and who was wrong.

Throughout the book the terms "slab block" and "perimeter block" appear. The slab block is a form of building, usually housing, that stands free of its neighbors and the streets that surround it. It is generally a simple rectangular box and is amenable to arrangement in repetitive rows. It is a principal component of many examples of the City of Hope. The perimeter block is more complex and can adapt to a variety of site conditions and topography. Its most important feature is that it can bend around corners and create continuous street frontage in all directions, and courtyards within. When perimeter blocks contain housing, the corner units assume special importance for an overall block or neighborhood design. Perimeter blocks are necessary to define street corridors as public pedestrian spaces and are an essential component of the Continuous City.

Architecture and urbanism have political dimensions, but it is astonishing how promiscuous the political embraces of both the Ruptured City and the Continuous City have been. The Ruptured City has at various times stood as an iconic symbol for the liberal social welfare state in the capitalist West, for Soviet Communism before and after Stalin, and for the awakening of the capitalist spirit in Communist China. The Continuous City has been the emblem for Social Democrats, Euro-Communists, Italian Fascists, and Nazis (in small towns especially) and during the Stalinist era in the USSR. Le Corbusier pedaled his wares in the Soviet Union and in Vichy France, and partially because he never consummated a deal in either place, he was welcomed as a player in postwar leftist France with the same goods for sale.

The twentieth and twenty-first centuries' struggles between the new and not completely new are parallel to, but surprisingly independent of, the great historical struggles between the Left and the Right, and between Enlightenment rationalism and the darker cosmologies. While it is not possible to attribute tens of millions of deaths directly to the clash of ideas about urbanism, this clash—our clash—has been as bitter, vicious, and consequential as the ideological and economic collisions that have taken the world to war.

The Ruptured City of Hope and the Continuous City of Love should not be judged for their political associations, which have proved to be contingent, temporary, and expedient, but only on the quality of life they sustain, and their capacity to provide a home for the vast populations of the world's cities. Severing ideas about the city from their political sponsorship has been a hard leap for many, but as we will see, there are urban treasures to be found in the darkest parts of the twentieth century.

Othello Station public housing reconstruction, Seattle, Daniel Solomon Design Partners
with Cornelia Oberlander Landscape Architect
Photo ©Tim Griffith

CHAPTER 2
The Story

The struggle between the City of Love and the City of Hope has a minidrama within it, an epic within an epic, fought on the battlefield of American public housing. The chronology that follows is a summary of the plot line. This could be a juicy screenplay, or perhaps it should be the libretto for a historical opera, like John Adams's *Nixon in China*.

The opera form seems apropos, because, like *Nixon in China*, it is a story driven by gigantic real characters. In our case the protagonists are not so well known as Adams's famous sextet: Richard Nixon, Pat Nixon, Henry Kissinger, Mao Tse-tung, Chou En Lai, and Jiang Ching. But our characters' dominance of a piece of history, and the huge effect their personal interactions had on the world, are dramatic in the same way.

In this telling of the story, much of the plot revolves around a central character, Catherine Bauer, later Catherine Bauer Wurster, widely regarded as the most passionate and eloquent voice on behalf of publicly funded housing for America's poorest citizens. Historical narratives sometimes benefit from gossip, and Bauer's life is the stuff of irresistible gossip. She was an immense energy—a "weapon" loaded with shells forged in Europe and aimed at America. These were shells in the sense of both cannon and canon—explosive, destructive, and also containing a rigid orthodoxy of prescription. Something happened to those "canon" shells on their trajectory across the Atlantic; what was loaded in them in Europe came out mutated and more lethal in American air.

Catherine Bauer and friend

Catherine Bauer was somewhat like Le Corbusier, an incandescent presence whose legacy is so baleful that it created the need for its very own counterreformation (of which I have been a part). To her great credit, she was a person with the ruthless intelligence to see, at the end of her life, the tragedy in her own flawed triumph. Le Corbusier's unassailable megalomania spared him the pain of a similar epiphany.

An important figure in Bauer's life was the great cultural historian and architectural critic Lewis Mumford. In searching his immense vocabulary for the correct term to describe his long relationship with Bauer, Mumford came up with the phrase "my doxy."[1] I have never known a man who referred to his lover as his doxy, let alone in a love letter (doxy is an especially salacious archaic term for a prostitute). It is hard to say which is more foreign to a twenty-first-century sensibility, the noun or the possessive pronoun that precedes it. "My doxy," my goodness.

Well, doxy or not, Catherine Bauer did get around. Her circle was the elite of planning and architecture on both sides of the Atlantic. Her trail of encounters left her with devoted and loving friends (including Mumford) to the end of her days and beyond. Bauer believed that among her European chums of the early 1930s, she was present at the dawn of a golden moment of progress for mankind: scientific rationalism about daylight, health, and housing production replacing the antiquated conventions of European and American cities. She unleashed her prodigious energies as a missionary for these ideas in ways that left deep marks on American cities for more than half a century. As our drama reaches its later phases, this author appears on stage, first as a supernumerary, just part of crowd scenes, but with a good view of the proceedings, then later as a minor character with a small but recurrent speaking part. These thrilling appearances, however trifling, in a large historical drama account for my preoccupation with telling this story over and over in different ways.

For the last twenty-odd years my partners and I have been intermittently enmeshed in rebuilding public housing that Catherine Bauer initiated. We have helped convert projects from a Ruptured City / City of Hope model that failed utterly and tragically, to a Continuous City model that has yet to receive the full test of time. This work continues, with the hope that what we learned from hope's failure is enabling us to do better than hope. The following chronology lists highlights of the long journey that housing for America's poor has made in the last ninety years:

1928   *Catherine Bauer (age twenty-two) publishes her first article on European modern housing in the* New York Times Magazine.

1930   *Catherine Bauer begins her long love affair and lifelong friendship with Lewis Mumford.*

1930   *Catherine Bauer returns to Europe with many introductions from Mumford, attends a housing seminar in Frankfurt, meets Ernst May, sees and loves the Romerstadt Zeilenbau.*

1931   *Bauer meets Philadelphia architect and Zeilenbau (slab block) enthusiast Oscar Stonorov.*

1932   *Another Bauer study trip on European social housing results in a prize-winning essay for* Fortune *magazine.*

1934   *Stonorov's Zeilenbau design for Carl Mackley Houses in Philadelphia is shown in a major Museum of Modern Art housing exhibition in New York; Bauer contributes a catalog essay.*

1934   *Bauer publishes the book* Modern Housing, *establishing her as the most eloquent spokesperson for a permanent federal public housing program based on European models. The essential idea of the book establishes conflict between the American city and rational, scientific habitat.*

1935   *Landmark Carl Mackley Houses are built to Alfred Kastner's semiperimeter block design, not Stonorov's Zeilenbau or slab block. Though Stonorov is usually credited, his partner Kastner's design is fundamentally different from his. The difference between these two schemes is central to* Modern Housing *(see chapter 9, "Hybrid 1").*

1937   *After years of bitter controversy, Congress passes the Wagner/Steagall Act establishing American public housing. The bill, originally drafted by Bauer, is finally passed in underfunded and much-amended form by a Republican-controlled Congress intent on ensuring its failure. Bauer succeeds in her goal in divorcing public housing from the dense fabric of cities on isolated sites, but fails to achieve funding that could emulate her European models.*

1938   *Catherine Bauer marries San Francisco architect William Wurster.*

1941   *Philadelphia's famous city planner Edmund Bacon, a close friend of Stonorov's, has a daughter named Elinor.*

1943   *Catherine Bauer and William Wurster have a daughter whom they name Sophie, apparently after Sophie Mumford, Lewis Mumford's wife during and after the years of his affair with Catherine.*

1943   *The Wagner/Steagall Act is finally implemented on a massive scale as emergency war worker housing in many cities including San Francisco, Seattle, and Los Angeles.*

1946   *Emergency war worker housing becomes "temporary" public housing but with minor renovations remains in use for the next sixty to seventy years.*

1948   *T. J. Kent and Mel Scott publish* New City: San Francisco Redeveloped, *a Euromodernist template for postwar San Francisco.*[2]

1949   *San Francisco establishes a well-funded redevelopment agency with powers of eminent domain.*

1950   *With a boost from wife Catherine and her influential friends, William Wurster becomes dean at UC Berkeley.*

1953–54 *Superficial retrofits and expansion of wartime housing projects occur throughout the country.*

1955–65 *In the name of slum clearance and urban renewal, the San Francisco Redevelopment Agency acquires and demolishes large areas of Victorian houses in the middle of the city, dispersing thousands of African American residents or relocating them to the already collapsing wartime public housing on the periphery.*

1960 *Wurster invites Mumford to Berkeley as Distinguished Visiting Professor. Wurster and Mumford collaborate on a master plan for housing at Stanford's Escondido Village. Wurster's office designs the buildings.*

1961 *Stanford undergraduate Daniel Solomon visits a bored and grumpy Professor Lewis Mumford during office hours, seeking advice on graduate schools to study both architectural design and architectural history. Mumford provides brilliant advice, most regrettably not taken, to apply to the Royal Academy in Copenhagen to study with Sten Eiler Rasmussen.*

Lewis Mumford

1963 *Oscar Stonorov, who helped introduce her to European social housing, sculpts the bust of Catherine Bauer.*

1964 *Daniel Solomon, a junior architect for Lawrence Halprin, is working in the Wurster office when Catherine Bauer Wurster mysteriously disappears. After a dramatic search she is found dead on Mount Tamalpais the next day.*

1968 *First-year assistant professor Daniel Solomon is summoned to the office of Dean William Wheaton. With a well-concealed tongue in cheek, Dean Wheaton castigates a terrified Professor Solomon for failing ever to call a meeting of the Wurster Hall Public Spaces Committee, of which Solomon had been appointed chair. Wheaton offers*

a way to make amends. He unveils the Stonorov bust of Catherine Bauer Wurster (the second casting is the centerpiece in the lobby of the Department of Housing and Urban Development in Washington, DC). Wheaton explains that he is dying of leukemia but wants to be able to kiss Catherine on the forehead each evening for as long as he can. He hands Professor Solomon a tape measure, asks him to measure the height of his own lips above the floor, then to measure Catherine and have an appropriately sized base fabricated for her effigy.

1969   *The Brookes Amendment to the Housing Act. Congress provides the final ingredient for public housing disaster, making isolated, already collapsing projects the exclusive domain of the poorest of the poor—almost all African American in many places.*

1971   *San Francisco redevelopment director Justin Herman dies of a heart attack two weeks after being strangled at a public meeting by an irate citizen protesting demolitions and forced relocation of African Americans from the center of the city. He never recovered from the attack.*

1972   *San Francisco Mayor Joseph Alioto, in response to citizen outcry, refuses federal highway funds to continue construction of elevated highways in the city.*

1977   *Daniel Solomon designs Pacific Heights Townhouses, setting a template for future work—his own and others.*

1978   *Daniel Solomon authors "Change without Loss" for the San Francisco Department of City Planning. It becomes the basis for a comprehensive rewrite of sections of the city's planning code.*

1981   *Venice Bienalle comes to San Francisco; see chapter 5, "Roots Sprout."*

1992   *The author and others found the Congress for the New Urbanism (CNU) and draft its charter.*

1992   *President Bill Clinton appoints Henry Cisneros as Secretary of HUD.*

1993   *After a shocking tour of HUD projects, Cisneros pronounces public housing a national disgrace and vows to tear down and replace hundreds of aging and distressed Wagner/Steagall projects.*

1994   *With much flourish—fender flags aflutter—Cisneros attends the Congress for the New Urbanism in Charleston, signs its charter, and promises to rebuild America's public housing according to the principles outlined in the charter (coauthored and edited by this author with many contributors).*

1995   *Cisneros convenes 400 HUD officials at Harvard to learn principles of new urbanism from the authors of the charter.*

1995   *Personal scandal forces Cisneros to resign. Clinton appoints Andrew Cuomo as secretary of HUD. Cuomo recruits Elinor Bacon to direct the HOPE VI Program to rebuild public housing. Bacon embraces CNU Charter principles as criteria for funding and begins the process of demolishing and replacing Wagner/Steagall Act housing nationwide.*

1998   *Carl Mackley Houses are placed on the National Register of Historic Places.*

1998   *Undergraduate Tolya Pfeffer-Bacon, daughter of Elinor, visits Professor Daniel Solomon during office hours, seeking advice on graduate schools.*

1999   *Daniel Solomon Design Partners wins the competition to partially demolish and add eight new dormitory buildings to Stanford's Escondido Village, originally designed by Wurster with Mumford.*

1999   *Undergraduate Otto Stonorov, grandnephew of Oskar, visits Professor Daniel Solomon during office hours, seeking advice on graduate schools. He has designed and built a complex and exquisite boat himself. On the basis of this exceptional project, Professor Solomon recommends him for Berkeley admission.*

2004   *Recent Wurster Hall graduates Tolya Pfeffer-Bacon and Otto Stonorov marry.*

2007   *Daniel Solomon Design Partners receives the commission for a HOPE VI* to rebuild public housing originally built on the wartime Wagner/Steagall model at Holly Park in Seattle. Solomon hires Cornelia Oberlander as landscape architect. Her husband, Peter Oberlander, had just published* Houser, *the definitive biography of Catherine Bauer.*

2009–   *Daniel Solomon and his partners redesign and rebuild Wagner/Steagall Act public housing in Seattle, San Francisco, Milwaukee, and Los Angeles.*

The narrative arc of this drama hinges on Bauer's youthful journeys—their timing and cast of characters, what she saw, what she focused on, and what she ignored.

She arrived in Europe at a crucial moment of transition.

The housing needs in Europe after WWI were colossal. There were many experiments; by 1930 an

New Amsterdam perimeter blocks

enormous amount had been built, and in that year a radical new idea was in the air. Through her many new friends on this trip, she was swept into the enthusiasm this idea generated in France, Germany, Sweden, Switzerland, and Holland—notably not in Italy, but we will go there soon.

One of the books that should be a design primer for students of urbanism is a fat, fifteen-pound volume called *The Atlas of the Dutch Urban Block*.[3] This magnificently produced book documents the virtuosity

---

*There is irony and paradox here, because Cisneros's great program of reconstruction bore the name HOPE VI. What HOPE VI intended and partially accomplished was deliverance for the inhabitants of public housing from the hopelessness engendered by what this book calls the City of Hope.

of the Dutch, particularly HP Berlage, in the years just before and after WWI in creating beautifully designed perimeter blocks of social housing. They were the best.

Then suddenly around 1930, the leading Dutch architects abandoned the model they had refined to absolute perfection and started building open blocks—slab blocks, or what Ernst May and others in Germany called Zeilenbau. In Germany, Bruno Taut, a great master in the period when modernism had not yet turned into rigid conventions, also turned toward this new idea of autonomous slab blocks. His new Berlin projects were on Bauer's itinerary.

For Bauer, the decisive event occurred in Frankfurt, where she attended a three-day seminar led by the Zeilenbau's chief apostle, Ernst May, and saw his spectacular new project, Romerstadt Siedlung. That was all it took. She believed, as many in Europe believed, that she was present at the dawn of a golden moment of progress for mankind: scientific rationalism replacing the antiquated conventions and layered irrationalities of European and American cities. She swallowed the whole fish as it was first presented in its pristine perfection—the new anti-city orthodoxy that was sweeping northern Europe. She brought this treasure home with her as the basis for her seminal book *Modern Housing.*[4] The essential idea of her book is the unresolvable conflict between the American city with its street grids, small blocks and lots, and patterns of land ownership on the one hand, and rational, scientific, humane habitat on the other. Modern social housing should not be urban infill for simple reasons

Pure Zeilenbau slab blocks, Zurich, 1930

of geometry, and because of the cost and messiness of acquisition, relocation, and land assembly; modern housing demanded large sites unencumbered by history, away from dense urban centers. Abundant and equal daylight for housing became both the emblem and the means of achieving a healthy, progressive, egalitarian society.

Her great hope was harnessing the political power and interventionist spirit of the New Deal to achieve in America what she saw as the coming new vision for Europe—finally realized, on a massive scale after WWII in the '50s and '60s as the French Grand Ensemble around Paris.

After the publication of *Modern Housing*, there are different accounts of what happened to European housing ideas on their transatlantic trip. According to her main biographer, Peter Oberlander, in his book *Houser*,[5] she becomes like Joan of Arc on a heroic quest through the labyrinth of Washington and the politics of labor unions. The result of her quest was the triumphant passage of the Wagner/Steagall Act, creating American public housing in 1937, enshrining the idea of large housing estates on the Zeilenbau model as a new piece of the New Deal.

Well, some of that did happen, notably William Lescaze's Williamsburg Houses in Brooklyn—a sort of fake Zeilenbau—an anti-city superblock with a diagonal twist for the parallel rows of apartments. The twist had no environmental logic and in fact turned the spaces between buildings into wind tunnels. It just looked European and modern, in pugnacious defiance of the Brooklyn fabric around it.

A more nuanced telling of Bauer's story by Gail Radford in *Modern Housing for America*[6] portrays the passage of Wagner/Steagall not as a triumph, but as a terrible defeat masquerading as victory for the housing lobby she led. The year 1937 was the low point for FDR and the New Deal. Republicans in Congress were passionately opposed to publicly funded and publicly owned housing for the poor, and so they eviscerated funding for Wagner/Steagall while passing it, ensuring the catastrophic failure of what was built. Bauer's advocacy succeeded in banishing public housing from the dense fabric of cities to isolated sites, but she failed utterly in funding it at a level that could emulate her iconic European models. The cheapest possible design and construction, inadequate operating budgets, site plans totally different from American cities, and big, isolated sites began the perfect recipe for disaster.

The final ingredient for the disaster came in the 1969 Brooke Amendments to the Housing Act, cosponsored by Republican Edward Brooke and Democrat Walter Mondale. The law gave preference to very-low-income residents and effectively chased families with employed workers out of public housing. It made these isolated, already-collapsing projects the exclusive domain of the poorest of the poor—almost all African American in many places. Gang culture, the drug economy, and mass incarceration of black youth followed the decay of projects.

Twenty-five years later Henry Cisneros surveyed the wreckage of the ruptured City of Hope and a new era began.

Robert Taylor Homes, public housing, Chicago

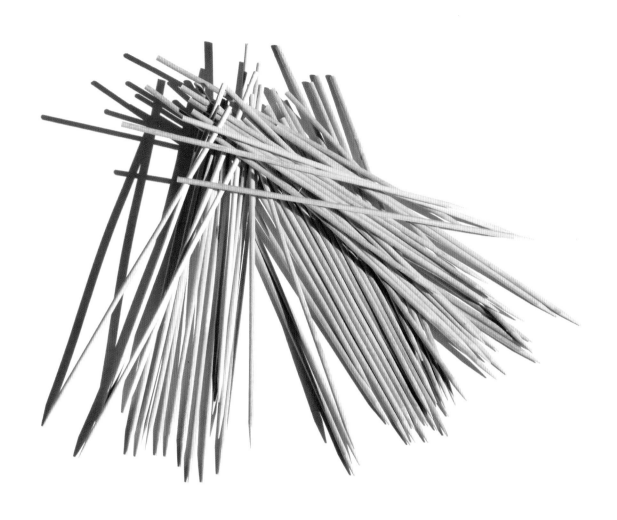

CHAPTER 3
Thinghood

Most architects suffer from an affliction that can turn them unwittingly into a menace, even to cities they profess to love. It is normal for people who are susceptible to the dream of being an architect to get bitten by this insidious bug when they are young. Sometimes they are little kids; most often they are in that confusing limbo between childhood and adulthood known as college. What hooks them is the amazing, life-shaping experience of making something in a methodical, disciplined way for the first time. Almost always, the act of seduction is the making of a *thing*—not making a party, not making a play, not making a garden. A thing, not an environment, narrative, or place—the distinction is important. The making of things and the City of Hope are close siblings, and the fate of each is entwined with the other. As we proceed, we will see more of this fierce bond of siblinghood.

My own story is typical, and it fits ever so neatly into the historical chronology of the last chapter. By the age of twenty I had come to think that architects were cool and arty and somehow connected to the great splendors of the world. Nothing else had seized hold of my future, so I felt compelled to try an introductory design course. After the very first assignment, that was it; my life plan was settled.

That first assignment was a simple enough, kindergartenish task, one conceived so that failure was unlikely, success probable. The instructor was a youngish guy named Tom Williamson, and he was the embodiment of what I thought an architect was supposed to be like—lean, sensitive looking, hair a little longer than was the fashion—a gestalt somewhere between stylish and bohemian scruffy. He liked to name-drop famous buildings and beautiful places he had been, which I thought was very cool. He showed us an enormous green book, a volume of *Sweets Architectural File*—a materials catalog that must have weighed about fifteen pounds. The task was to purchase a box of toothpicks and make a structure from them that would both span over the catalog and support its weight.

I started by laying toothpicks end to end to make a circle around the template of the catalog. I discovered that by gluing little clusters of six toothpicks together, I could make tetrahedrons. I then had the bright idea that if I made lopsided tetrahedrons all around the circle, they could eventually go together and make a dome. I didn't have the math skills to figure out how different the lengths of toothpicks needed to be to get the tetrahedrons lopsided in the right way, so I did it by trial and error. Lots of toothpicks, lots of glue, lots of trial, and lots of error, but eventually, after multiple sleepless nights and skipped classes, it worked. I had made a sort of geodesic dome (a term unknown to me), and it was strong as a house.

My dome was perfect. I had made perfection. Tom Williamson said so, and he imagined it as a big building where one could walk beneath the splendid points of the overhanging tetrahedrons. I was completely hooked. Oh, how I loved my toothpick dome; Brunelleschi could not have loved his more.

Soon, I came to see (as one was taught to see) that the great architects of the day were toothpick dome makers par excellence. They had the perfectibility of objects down pat: they could create all-of-a-piece, perfect, Platonic things. Perfect and consistent, one idealized thing, inside and out. Kahn could do it, Mies could do it, Frank Lloyd Wright could do it, and, son-of-a bitch, I could do it—just give me a shot. That is the standard architecture student epiphany.

Thinghood—the autonomy and integrity of building form is the main idea I was taught in architecture school. In itself, it is not something bad. Quite the contrary. It is why we revere the buildings of all of the modern masters. Structure and space, pipes and structure, use and geometry—all congruent, all fitting together, perfectly, seamlessly.

In this view of buildings, they are not different in kind from other sorts of objects, like toasters, bicycles, or race cars. Buildings can be beautiful in just the ways that those other things can be. The difference is that buildings, unlike other objects, are the constituent elements of cities, but cities are not simply aggregations of toasters, bicycles, and race cars. The city is a meta-artifact composed of artifacts, but not simply like toys in a box. The city has its own complex and transformative logic that shapes the nature of the things that compose it. The city is an organism that tolerates many things, but not all things. The city is tough and resilient, but not infinitely so. Cities can be damaged and, like other organisms, they can be killed by the things within them.

An undergraduate with his tube of glue and box of toothpicks doesn't worry about these matters. He also doesn't realize that the box contains a hidden message enlisting him in the vast project of the Enlightenment, now into its third century and still soldiering on, despite generations of postmodern skepticism. The message is about the redemptive power of reason, the rational shaping of the world, the perfectibility of things, progress, a better day to come—all in a box of toothpicks. Skepticism may come later for many reasons, but it will never completely outshine that thrilling moment when the little dome held up the giant catalog without so much as a wince. The perfectibility of toothpicks is both immanent and utopian. Buildings can be the embodiment of perfectibility, a palpable triumph of the rational. The best buildings are little utopias and their architects are little utopians. But does the perfectibility of many small things imply the perfectibility of everything? Do lots of little utopias make one big one? Maybe it is better not to ask the question and just do for the world what one can.

Better not to ask the question because it has already been answered, resoundingly, all over the world. The big utopian project of the ruptured modernist city was a giant bust a long time ago—at Brasilia, at Chandigarh, in the catastrophe of American urban renewal, all over Europe. These days, Le Corbusier's Plan Voisin for Paris, replacing the beautiful Sixteenth Arrondissement with a grid of identical skyscrapers, is taken to be either a tongue-in-cheek media stunt of its day or the ranting of a madman. In the great battle of Jane Jacobs versus the Athens Charter of Le Corbusier (the Koran of modernist town planning), the result was Jane by a knockout decades ago. Just ask any city planner what it is they believe in. The answer is likely to be in paragraph-long block quotes (or near paraphrases if they don't quite have it straight) from *Death and Life of Great American Cities*.

Strangely, the universally acknowledged failure of big utopias has left little utopias largely unscathed. Big utopians are perceived as fools, but the rewards for making little utopias remain pervasive, tangible, and immediate. People say nice things about you. If you are a student of architecture, it starts with your first student jury and, if you play your cards right, it continues through a lifetime, with fancier and fancier people saying nicer and nicer things. Even after you're dead. For many a twenty-year-old, it certainly appears to be something worth trying for. But some kids are better toothpick gluers than others. Kids who give smashing parties, or cook well, or tell funny stories aren't necessarily clever at making things. The good gluers were the ones who stuck it out through the purgatory of architecture school. Graduation was the triumph of the thing makers. These days, fancy new software has replaced toothpicks and glue, but those things on the luminous screen are even more disembodied from the world than the toothpicks of yore.

A perfect thing demands a perfect place to put the thing. It was a great frustration that my student apartment, shared with three messy guys, never provided the right setting for my beautiful dome. Not the mantel (too small), not the coffee table (too much stuff), nowhere in my shared bedroom. The white Formica kitchen table worked fine for display when it was clean and empty, but it kept being preempted for lesser uses, such as eating. In the white gallery used as a jury room, it had looked so smashing, but not so out in the mess of the world.

The mess of the world is a big problem for thing makers. These days it is rare to find someone who still takes seriously the twentieth-century proposition that the great cities of the world should be cleaned and emptied to make room for a new rationalist utopia. That idea is finally discredited beyond redemption, but all over the world the irreconcilable ill fit between the form of buildings and the form of the continuous city is still with us. It's the thinghood thing. The love of thinghood is the unifying theme, modern architecture's main idea, the bond that unites the shards, the blobs, the shiny boxes, and the latest parametric warpages. Thinghood is somewhat like manhood—a point of pride, something to be asserted and defended, and something male adolescents think is terrific. It is why Rem Koolhaas is so fond of the pithy epithet *fuck context*.

Photo ©Fred Lyon

CHAPTER 4

Roots: Fred Lyon and Anne Vernez-Moudon to the Years of Rupture

In the 1940s and '50s, the great photographer Fred Lyon captured the soul of San Francisco. He recorded the people of the time: stevedores, socialites, bums, ordinary Joes, white, black, Chinese —everybody. He recorded the dense neighborhoods that spill over the hills, the exuberant wooden architecture, the city's amazing play of light and fog. Most poetically he captured children using the steep streets and hidden parts of the city as an enchanted playground. I was one of those children.

The Way It Was[1] is the title Lyon gave to a 2014 book of his early photographs of the city. These photographs are to San Francisco somewhat like Giambattista Nolli's famous map of 1748 is to Rome—a definitive record of the city intact, as it was before the interventions of the modern world. In the 1950s San Francisco was a place that had grown for a century according to its founding principles, interrupted only briefly by the 1906 earthquake and fire. In the century from 1850 to 1950, no one acted on the idea that there was something wrongheaded about the way San Francisco was laid out. Daniel Burnham did have his own vision of how the city should have been, but his grandiose plan of 1905 was completely ignored after the earthquake and fire. After 1950, it was another matter. The Ruptured City came to town in a big way, but it took a while for the scars to appear, and all during my childhood the whole city looked just like Fred Lyon's magical photographs.

Flash forward to the late 1960s and 1970s. I was a young assistant professor at Berkeley, teaching with Anne Vernez-Moudon, who later became a distinguished urban design professor at the University of Washington. She is French/Swiss, a European at heart, and often took advantage of the academic summer to travel in Europe and check out the scene. By the mid-1970s, she knew about ideas and people I had never heard of: *Tendenza, typologia, Muratori, Caniggia.*

In those days she was at work on the classic book on San Francisco, *Built for Change.*[2] Her book combines ideas she learned in Italy and the Netherlands with a decidedly Anglo-American clarity of thought and prose. With a complete absence of florid Italianate pedantry, she dissects the interaction between the city's methods of land division, its topography, and its characteristic form of buildings. She tells the story of how San Francisco was built and why it is the way it is (or was).

Anne Vernez-Moudon's book and Fred Lyon's photographs are two completely different, but totally complementary, modes of observation of the beautiful city I grew up in.

Before her book was published in its final form in 1982, I realized that something was terribly wrong. The San Francisco of Fred Lyon and Anne Vernez-Moudon was actually disappearing. Something was eating away at the mysterious, foggy city of my childhood, the place where John Huston and Alfred Hitchcock made movies and where Dashiell Hammett set his stories of intrigue and darkness. Those sinister, misty lanes where Sam Spade hunted for Myles Archer's killer in *The Maltese Falcon* were being erased, one by one.

Slowly I began to understand the illness and see its source. The disease (it was a disease) consisted of the very things that architecture school had programmed me and my peers to believe in—the City of Hope. My master's thesis of 1966 was an apotheosis—a city-be-damned, megalomaniacal megastructure that wiped out most of the San Francisco waterfront, including A. Page Brown's beloved Ferry Building. It is worth noting where 1966 falls in the chronology of chapter 2. This was the heyday of the City of Hope in San Francisco.

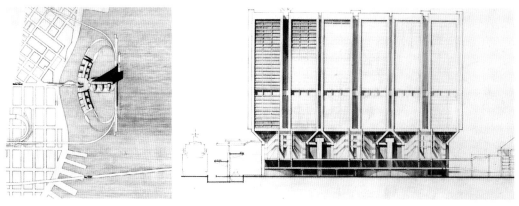

Daniel Solomon's UC Berkeley master's thesis, 1966

My master's thesis was a gigantic act of architectural masturbation that attempted, to the best of my limited abilities, to outdazzle Giovanni Battista Piranesi, Antonio Sant'Elia, and Kenzo Tange all at once. In my own plea of innocence, I can justly claim that I was only doing what almost every other aspiring architect in the world was doing in 1966. The fantastical graphic musings of Archigram, Archizoom, and Super Studio were in the air or about to be.

My graduate student's fantasy was simply a more grandiose version of what planners and architects had already been doing to San Francisco for fifteen years. My town, San Francisco, like almost everywhere else, had committed itself to the Ruptured City of Hope after WWII.

The New City (green layer) vs. San Francisco (black layer);
Mel Scott and T. J. Kent, 1948

Our local version of the City of Hope was first articulated in 1948 in a visionary plan called the New City, by two authors of great local stature: Mel Scott, the city's first planning director and T. J. Kent, the first chairman of City and Regional Planning at UC Berkeley. It described the Victorian fabric of the city in language that could have been lifted from a 1950s horror movie trailer:

In this new city of space and living green there are no densely built up blocks. Here no families live in murky cubicles, damp basements, rooms that are hardly more than closets. Public health nurses find no overcrowded households, no children or young people sleeping in the same room with victims of tuberculosis. Nor do building inspectors discover unvented heaters, termite riddled floors and walls . . . [3]

Gone are the disreputable joints, the so-called smoke shops, the "hotels" and pool hall hangouts known to police. Gone, too, are the alleys in which juvenile gangs plotted mischief that sometimes ended in murder.

What this lurid description is referring to is exactly the city that Fred Lyon recorded so lovingly, that Anne Vernez-Moudon analyzed so perceptively, and that film directors were haunted by. What Scott and Kent proposed was to raze it to the ground, to reduce film noir San Francisco to powder and replace as much as they could with what they show as a great swath of green ink with widely spaced slab buildings—Euro-modernism on giant superblocks, *Grand Ensemble* by the

Bay. With no place left to lurk, who knows what would happen to Dashiell Hammet's characters? Imagine Sidney Greenstreet in a jogging suit, adrift on the sea of green ink.

Unlike my master's thesis, the New City was more than masturbation. It bred living offspring from the city's new Redevelopment Agency, implementing federally funded urban renewal. During WWII, the center of the city had become the home for a large African American population, many lured from the rural South by shipyard jobs, and many crowded into Victorian houses vacated by the internment of Japanese Americans. These fragile wooden buildings had survived the Depression, the war years, the disenfranchisement of their owners, and the influx of rural poor. Most had not had a coat of paint in twenty years. The then-black Fillmore District in the heart of the city became ground zero for urban renewal: target number one.

A generation of Americans came back from the experience of winning WWII, euphoric at having survived the horror, intoxicated with accomplishment. Many were filled with hope, hubris, and personal ambition. They saw places like worn and tattered San Francisco as rotting putrescence to be wiped away, and as vast fields of opportunity. Undoubtedly, many conflated the new presence of African Americans with urban decay to be excised.

The acts of excision were the embrace of the Ruptured City; they took form in three separate sets of programs starting in earnest in the early 1950s, each lasting more than two decades. The fact that these initiatives were uncoordinated with one another and were each the province of narrowly focused, single-purpose public agencies was itself emblematic of the fracture.

First was urban renewal, based on the idea of "slum clearance," a popular element of federal housing policy since the Public Works Administration of the New Deal in 1935. As reinstated in Title I of the Housing Act of 1949, the federal government provided local redevelopment agencies a four-to-one match of federal dollars to "city share" for acquisition, demolition, and reconstruction of urban areas deemed "blighted." Eager inspectors from San Francisco's newly enfranchised redevelopment agency easily found conditions that met the criteria for blight in the district its African American citizens proudly called the Fillmore (or Feel'mo when they wanted to sound ethnic). The agency referred to it by its exhumed nineteenth-century name, the Western Addition, not a familiar term to San Franciscans at the time. The fact that the Fillmore was packed with architectural gems and was the West Coast's most vibrant center of black commerce and culture did nothing to distract the eyes of inspectors from rickety back stairs and old-fashioned electric meters. Blight, blight, blight—that was the incantation that unlocked the federal treasure chest. As a bitter survivor of the redevelopment blitz a half century ago puts it, the neighborhood rapidly became "the Feel'no'mo."

Western Addition A-1, an eighteen-block swath of demolition in the middle of the city, was the first implementation of the New City of 1948, with a couple of truly insidious twists added to it. With one mighty throw of a stone, the redevelopment agency took aim at several targets simultaneously, scoring multiple bull's-eyes. By using local money to transform part of one ordinary street in the city grid (Geary Street) into a grade-separated crosstown motorway, the agency qualified for the four-to-one federal match to acquire and demolish not only the initial eighteen blocks, but the additional sixty square blocks of Western Addition A-2. The fact that the high-speed motorway goes for less than a quarter mile, to and from nowhere in particular, never seemed to bother anyone involved.

I was in high school when the redevelopment bulldozer was being cranked up to full throttle. As a football and track jock of very modest talent at a large, one-third-black public school, I had many black athlete buddies who lived in the Fillmore. They liked to pile into my father's big Cadillac and order their white chauffeur (me) around the neighborhood. It was a great neighborhood, full of street life along Fillmore and Divisadero Streets and home to some of the country's best jazz clubs—Bop City, the Black Hawk, the Tin Angel. The royalty of the jazz world played those clubs:

Left to right: Amancio Ergina Village, 1984, ©Henry Bowles; Biedeman Place Townhouses, 1987, ©Jane Lidz

Billie, Dizzy, Miles, the best of the best. It was the Harlem Renaissance West. The Black Hawk had a section where they served food and soft drinks, so kids under twenty-one could commune with the giants. So, sadly, it all went away: the street life, the little businesses, the jazz clubs, most of the people, and seventy-eight blocks of architectural treasure—the Continuous City by every measure, brutally erased.

The eighteen blocks of A-1 were combined into superblocks and renamed Japantown as a gesture of atonement for the outrageous injustice of internment. The reconfiguration of blocks effectively disconnected the rapidly gentrifying white neighborhood to the north from the still largely African American blocks to the south, softening the harsh contrast of black and white with a lightly tinted Asian buffer. Apparently, these sorts of buffered transitions are easier on the eyes.

Residents of the Fillmore were dispersed, some to the ghetto suburb of East Palo Alto, many to remnant wartime housing built in great haste in 1943 for workers at the Hunters Point Naval Shipyard. Naturally, the destruction of a community of 2,500 households, including many large families, did not occur without a bitter struggle. In 1971, at a Western Addition community meeting, an irate citizen leapt across the speaker's table to strangle Justin Herman, the high-handed wheeling-and-dealing director of redevelopment. Herman died two weeks later of a heart attack, an important milestone recorded in chapter 2's chronology.

Things changed soon after that. By the time Western Addition A-2 was underway, the New City idea had completely lost its luster. My own later contributions to A-2, Amancio Ergina Village in 1984 and Biedeman Place Townhouses in 1987, were attempts to recover some of the spirit that redevelopment had destroyed. While redevelopment was in its aggressive years of "slum clearance," public housing authorities were busily producing their own version of the Ruptured City for the nation's poorest citizens. San Francisco had more than its share of the truly terrible public housing projects of that era, but we will return to that story in a later chapter.

I could not have known in 1965 that almost forty years later I would encounter some of the very people displaced from the Fillmore, and their children and grandchildren, who had been consigned ever since to a god-awful public housing gulag near Hunters Point. The chance to rebuild that terrible place was all the more meaningful to me because I knew and remembered so vividly what these families had lost.

The third piece of the rupture puzzle is what the Interstate Highway Act of 1949 had in store for American cities. The nature of a jigsaw puzzle depicting rupture is that none of the pieces fit together. So it was with urban renewal, public housing, and urban freeways—all occurring at the same time as parts of the same picture. The autonomy of the public agencies—Redevelopment Agency, Housing Authority, Division of Highways—each the domain of one-issue specialists— ensured that these activities had no relationship to each other or to the existing city. The new federally funded network of elevated freeways ripped through San Francisco as if it didn't exist—severing the city from its waterfront, tearing neighborhoods apart, defacing the front of the resplendent Beaux-Arts city hall building. More than anything else, it was the continuing expansion of the brutal freeway network that galvanized the citizens of San Francisco against the Ruptured City in all its manifestations.

By the 1970s there was lots of new building for San Franciscans to hate, and lots to fear about the future. Many neighborhoods had unthinkably gross infill buildings stuffed into them—new housing that followed the planning code but lacked the flavor of the old city entirely or blocked precious views. Neighborhood groups organized to stop speculators from demolitions and wrongly scaled, often hideous rebuilding, but it was the freeway expansion that created a political opposition with real teeth.

35

Like Jane Jacobs in her struggles against the mighty Robert Moses in New York, many San Franciscans discovered that bringing the Ruptured-City juggernaut to its knees was not only profoundly important, it was fun. People could meet their neighbors, go to meetings, bang on tables, and wear funny hats. African Americans could join WAPAC (the Western Addition Project Area Committee), act really, really black, and scare the hell out of white folk.

And the best part was—it worked.

In a spectacular performance at a televised hearing of the Senate Highway Appropriations subcommittee, San Francisco's colorful and combative mayor Joe Alioto, unintimidated by the powerful senators controlled by the giant highway lobby, eloquently refused federal dollars to complete the freeway network. Then in 1972, the new mayor, George Moscone, appointed a planning commission consisting entirely of neighborhood activists who had organized the anti-freeway campaign.

Moscone's new planning commission took an extreme measure, imposing interim controls and downzoning across the city that brought virtually all housing production to a halt. This occurred when the city was robust with job growth and new office buildings, setting off a process of housing inflation that has never abated.

All this coincided with my own first efforts to try to build a tiny, quite innocent infill housing project in the city. I discovered that it was impossible because of the interim controls, which I thought were restrictive to the point of craziness. I voiced my dismay to a staff planner, who agreed, and suggested that, since I was teaching at Berkeley, I involve the UC Department of Architecture to help write better controls.

With some small grants from the National Endowment for the Arts, I became the planning department's de facto consultant with some graduate student assistants, one of whom was Thomas Gordon Smith, later an influential dean at Notre Dame. Starting in 1975, we did case studies in graduate studios of new housing dotted through San Francisco neighborhoods, and we prepared a report with the catchy title "Change without Loss." It was influenced by Anne Vernez-Moudon's observations of the city grid, topography, lot platting, and building types and resulted in extensive rewriting of the San Francisco planning code in 1978.

This process involved many public meetings, and I met an ambitious young lawyer named Alex Najjar, who suggested using a site that he controlled on the edge of the fancy Pacific Heights neighborhood as a demonstration project, since our proposed controls permitted substantially more density than the interim rules. The Pacific Heights Association and the planning

Pacific Heights Townhouses, 1978

department went along with this suggestion, and I was able to design my first fourteen-unit San Francisco project, Pacific Heights Townhouses.

Pacific Heights Townhouses was an anomaly—a work by a young architect actually related to its context (not a term in common usage)—accompanied by some analysis of that context and new ideas about planning laws and zoning. Then as now, the principal interest of the architectural press was novelty, and Pacific Heights Townhouses and its analytical background qualified as a novelty at the time. It was a new project that the preservationists actually liked. Even California's historian laureate, Kevin Starr, commented that it had captured the feeling of the city. *Progressive Architecture*, then the leading American professional journal, gave it six pages and the cover.

Not long after the publication of Pacific Heights Houses and completion of several other projects, I was invited to talk at Columbia's School of Architecture, as a recent graduate of promise. While in New York I was asked also to give the same talk at Cooper Union. Columbia was familiar turf and not so scary, but Cooper Union, with its famous and formidable dean, John Hedjuk, was a bit terrifying. At Cooper, Hedjuk himself greeted me in all his massive presence, brought me to the lecture room, listened to my talk, and, when I was done, imperiously directed me back to his office. To my astonishment, he had notes and vigorous opinions about all the work. He said never to design a restaurant again (I had done two). Restaurants and the various commercial environments I had attempted were an invitation to vulgarity. Hedjuk thought I had taken Robert Venturi's championing of the vulgar much more literally than Venturi himself had. My houses were okay, but any architect with some chops can do nice houses. But the housing in San Francisco, and all that business with the city maps, he said, with that you are on to something. I had thought he would find the thinking behind Pacific Heights Townhouses and its two successor projects sentimental and predictable, and I hoped he would find the other things interesting, but I had it completely backward. I listened carefully to this remarkable man, this true teacher, and have lived by his words ever since.

It was a big moment.

La Strada Novissima, 1980 Venice Architecture Biennale

CHAPTER 5

Roots Sprout

Another Big Moment.

In 1980, the Venice Biennale made an international stir with an exhibition titled *Strada Novissima*, conceived and curated by Roman architect and historian Paolo Portoghesi. He invited each of thirty or so emerging stars of the postmodern architectural firmament to design and build a full-scale, three-story façade out of temporary materials to be assembled along both sides of a mock traditional street inside the vast Venice Arsenale. The facades by Leon Krier, Aldo Rossi, Ricardo Bofill, and other luminaries were inventive and for the most part well done, and their collective impact was a powerful polemic against the anti-street, antihistorical Ruptured City modernist orthodoxy then dominating city design all over Europe.

This occurred just as San Francisco was emerging from its own traumatic Ruptured City episode, in which the streets and building fabric that gave the city its beloved character were considered an anachronism, something irretrievable from another time. A wealthy San Francisco couple were so moved by the exhibit, so convinced it was relevant at home, that they decided to underwrite transporting the entire Strada Novissima to an abandoned pier in San Francisco's Fort Mason in 1981. Someone—I don't know who—decided that four San Francisco architects should add facades to the exhibit and that I should be one of them. The others were the brilliant young firm of Mark Mack and Andrew Batey; William Turnbull, also an extraordinarily gifted small architect; and, to balance the three tiny firms, the San Francisco office of Skidmore Owings & Merrill. It was a weird selection, but I was thrilled and stunned to be included.

Each façade was about twenty feet wide and thirty feet high, leading to a little partitioned enclosure with an exhibition of the architect's work. My façade had twin towers of mock glass descending onto an arched portal with a vague reference to Vienna's great Karl Marx Hof—a historical pastiche appropriate to this American launch of postmodernism. Inside my little enclosure was a continuous row of identical picture frames with photographs, drawings, and city maps explaining the rationale for my first San Francisco projects—Pacific Heights Townhouses and three or four successor projects developing the same ideas.

On the morning before the evening the show was to open, it was still a big mess of frantic activity. My pavilion was done, but I had barely started organizing the long row of picture frames. I was working away on the dirty floor in jeans and a filthy T-shirt when famous people started traipsing through for a pre-opening look.

La Strada Novissima, 1981, Daniel Solomon

First came Tom Wolfe, by himself, in one of his signature impeccably pressed white suits. He barely noticed as he stepped over me on the floor, being careful not to soil himself. Next came the famous planner, author, and dean Jonathan Barnett, whom I recognized, though we had never met. He seemed a bit friendlier. As I continued to sit on the floor screwing frames together, he looked carefully at the images I had finished hanging, and he read all the text. He came over and introduced himself, and said, "I'm afraid you just don't understand the game. You must not have read everybody else's texts; you're much too lucid." It took me years of knowing droll Jonathan Barnett to understand that this was a compliment.

Then came a whole gaggle of fancy-looking people, led by Paolo Portoghesi himself. He had a beautiful sport coat over his shoulders, Roman fashion, with arms and sleeves operating independently. He was flanked by Philip Johnson, who, despite his animated speech and gestures, looked like he had died two years before. Portoghesi said nothing, but Johnson uttered what I took to be a harrumph of approval—"Who is this Dan Solomon?" They were followed by some reporters, one with an early camcorder and several striking and beautifully groomed women who stepped over me carefully. Finally, there was a tall Italian fellow with an aristocratic stoop who lingered, looking at the hung frames after the others moved on.

In an imperative voice he said, "Dan Solomon, stand up. Stand up now een thees moment. I give you *abraccio*," and he threw his arms around me: "You are my brother." This weird intro preceded a long, effusive monologue that was studded with names and terms I had heard uttered by Anne Vernez-Moudon: *Muratori, Caniggia, typologia*, and a phrase I had not heard before, *lotto gotico*. He pointed excitedly to the pictures and drawings of my work and said, "In thees moment, you *rebuiltited* the town." I came to learn that *rebuiltited* was one of his favorite words. So began a long friendship.

His name was Roberto Pirzio-Biroli, an architect from Udine near Venice, educated at Sapienza in Rome, a devoted protégé of Paolo Portoghesi, and a former student of Gianfranco Cannigia.

One of the things that Roberto responded to in the row of picture frames was a pair of figure/ground drawings of typical San Francisco blocks. Figure/ground drawings are black-and-white abstractions of building or city plans in which the buildings are depicted as solid black and everything else is the white of the page. They were introduced in the US as analytical tools in the 1970s by Colin Rowe in a famously influential urban design program at Cornell. A form of figure/ground drawings had long been fundamental to the pedagogy at Pirzio-Biroli's University of Rome, Sapienza; hence the gleam of recognition.

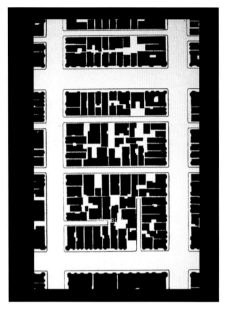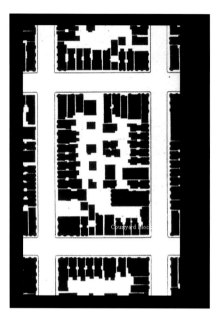

San Francisco block plans; drawings by John Ellis

Figure/ground drawings are depictions of the complex *pas de deux* that occurs in a city between buildings and open space. Once one learns to decode their messages, they tell a rich and detailed story about what places are like and how they came to be. The San Francisco figure/grounds that Roberto saw show one block of typical San Francisco row houses bisected by two alleys, and another block of similar buildings that has no alleys, but small courtyards between the buildings on the street and small cottages in the middle of the block. Little hairlines of the white page show through to delineate the lot lines between the black shapes of the separately owned buildings.

Many things come through in these drawings. First is the original city grid of blocks and its subdivision into lots (*lotto gotico*). Then one sees that the black shapes of the buildings are mostly similar, but not identical; they are a "type" and one can see what is typical about them. Most are the same width, and they vary slightly in length. All but the shortest ones have notches along their sides that represent light wells. The fronts of the buildings each have two protrusions that represent the paired bay windows so common in San Francisco. Some have bay windows on the back and some are flat across the back.

These two blocks are the same size and have the same building type, but one can "read" in the drawings that the blocks are quite different. Each is spatially complex and full of discovery; one can imagine exploring the streets, alleys, and courtyards—the white spaces between the black shapes. Perhaps the mysterious world of *The Maltese Falcon* is locked in these ink drawings. Imagine that exploration on a cool, foggy San Francisco night with lights reflecting on wet streets.

The black shapes are similar (a "type"), but not identical, except for occasional groups of three or four that are the same. One can deduce that most of the buildings were built one at a time, except when small builders sometimes acquired three or four adjacent lots. One can also "read" that the courtyards and alleys represent cleverness on the part of someone to cram more density on these blocks, using the same small building type—real-estate intelligence at work.

One can lose oneself in the stories that figure/ground drawings evoke. They enable you to see urbanism as a game, like chess, played within a grid of streets, blocks, and lots. Like chess, it is a game that can be played by beginners who know the basic rules, or with subtle, unpredictable complexity by a grand master. Trying to become a grand master is a complicated matter—a project for a lifetime.

Figure/ground drawings can show urban disintegration and mess as vividly and eloquently as they show coherence. They can depict the forces that shatter townscapes—buildings so big or so oddly shaped that the area around them is ripped apart; they show how shapeless open spaces can disrupt a neighborhood, or what big parking lots do to a city. You can easily see in figure/ground drawings how architects' obsessions with thinghood can damage the city. You can tell the difference instantly between a figure/ground of ruptured city sprawl and a figure/ground of the fabric of a beautiful city.

Grille extrudée

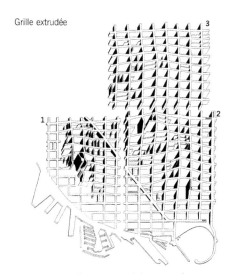

Florence Lipsky's conceptual drawing of San Francisco showing topography

As powerful a tool as these drawings are, they don't tell the whole story of anywhere, least of all San Francisco, with its extreme topography. Anne Vernez-Moudon's *Built for Change* is short on graphics that depict the story she tells about the interaction of land division, building type, and the steep hills. After its publication, a Berkeley PhD student, Florence Lipsky, took on the task of creating beautiful conceptual drawings in her own book, *Grids and Hills*, adding topography to Anne's more rudimentary diagrams.

With his Sapienza training, Pirzio-Biroli is a fluent reader of figure/grounds and all sorts of analytical drawings of cities. What he saw in my first San Francisco projects was the struggle to reconcile the patterns of the historic blocks with the modern conditions that tend to rip them apart.

If an architect lives in a place with an economy that supports new building, and if he manages to work for a long time without screwing up too badly or too publicly, he is likely to be entrusted with bigger and more complicated projects as he gets older. As projects get larger, literal replication of the old patterns and types becomes more and more impossible. Rules about fire exits, handicapped access, ever stricter energy codes, ever-larger financial entities, and the pressure for more and more density combine to create conditions that are fundamentally different from those that produced the old blocks.

The standard response in the world of architecture to these huge differences is that of the "post-urban" crowd at Harvard and elsewhere. They stand by their modernist grandfathers and great-grandfathers and say in their shrill, dogmatic way—just give up on the historic city. Forget it. Forget about Boston, San Francisco, or Rome. Forget about repairing them, let alone making new places anything like them. *Just get over it.*

Since those first projects that created the instant bond with Pirzio-Biroli, I have continued a journey fueled by San Francisco's onanistic love affair with itself. For a while this was a solo endeavor, but for a long time it has been a collaborative practice, slowly attracting larger and larger projects that make a case different from the dominant "post-urbanists." The message of this body of work is—it's not over, not nearly—it has just gotten harder. Achieving the Continuous City is not a simple matter of replicating historic buildings and blocks. That is indeed impossible. But assimilating those old forms deeply in one's soul lets them reemerge as something completely new. It involves a bit of skill, some practice, and a feel for the subject. It is not a matter of method or formula, because the game is different every time you play it. That is why it is endlessly interesting.

CHAPTER 6
A Reconstructed Diary

In 1951, at the age of eleven, I owned my first belted trench coat. When my family had dinner in San Francisco's North Beach, I liked it best when my father parked down near the ships amid the brick buildings, so solid and brooding on foggy nights. I thought I would grow up to be Sam Spade, and somewhere on the waterfront I would meet Sidney Greenstreet, Peter Lorre, and my ultimate dream creature, Lauren Bacall, who I knew was lurking, just there in the shadows.

In 1961 I treasured a thick black book called *Space, Time and Architecture.*[1] Architecture students in those days read and reread that book the way serious students of Islam read and reread the Koran. It was written at Harvard by the court historian of the modern movement, Sigfried Giedion. That year I produced an exhibition of photographs of San Francisco's newly constructed Embarcadero Freeway, which I loved because it embodied Giedion's big idea:

The essence of space as it is conceived today is its many-sidedness, the infinite potential for relations within it . . . In order to grasp the true nature of space the observer must project himself through it.

In 1971 I moved to North Beach, into a beautiful apartment with a garden off the Filbert steps that climb Telegraph Hill through an enchanted garden. It cost $140 a month, the same as I had been paying for a modest place in Berkeley. There were lots of choices of lovely places to live in the city at that price. Then, and for a long time afterward, I kept up a clandestine love affair with the Embarcadero Freeway, which was my way home from Berkeley where I taught:

Brakepoint . . . WHOOMP . . . downshift . . . power on . . . apex . . . full power . . . a little drift . . . a little correction . . .

Blasting down the Clay/Washington or Broadway off-ramps, usually late at night, no one ever caught me playing race car on the Embarcadero Freeway. From Giedion's kinetic observer to car freak was an easy transition.

In 1991, two years after the Loma Prieta earthquake, I wrote the following:

On the eve of its demolition, I walked the top deck of the freeway . . . It was drizzling and dark, and it was like walking in Venice, where the only sounds are footsteps and voices. For some reason there were lots of languages—Portuguese, German, Japanese, French, Chinese. People were in silhouette in the dark, just walking quietly, talking. As much as I had loved the views driving—10,000 times, 20,000 times—they were much more beautiful on foot, in the quiet. On February 27, 1991, the automobile era ended.

In 2001, my partners and I started working on the design of the first phase of Broadway Family Apartments on the very site where the Embarcadero Freeway knifed into North Beach. We nestled the buildings into the remnants of a block that had been torn asunder by the freeway. We created a new weave of courtyards and passages through the block to link the old and new buildings and the streets in interesting ways. In 2009, the first phase of the project was finally finished. The block is remade—denser, more complex, maybe better than before. Rents in the subsidized project are as modest as they were in North Beach fifty years ago, but in 2009, for each apartment there were 105 applicants: eighty-one apartments, more than 8,500 applicants. There is a new solid-brick building where an old one stood before the freeway took its place. If on a foggy night the building appears to brood a little, that is okay, because it may help return the city to a state in which eleven-year-olds can imagine their dream creatures lurking in the shadows.

Broadway Family Apartments, San Francisco
Photo ©Tim Griffith

CHAPTER 7

On Deceit

"Truth is so precious, she should always be attended by a bodyguard of lies."[1]

—WINSTON CHURCHILL

Churchill made this remark (to the great amusement of his dinner companion, Stalin) at the Yalta Conference of 1944, during the last stages of planning for Overlord, the Allied invasion of Western Europe. Both Churchill and Stalin delighted in paradox, irony, and blasphemy, and despite their titanic differences, they truly enjoyed each other's company. They both knew that the success of the invasion, the very survival of the first waves of troops, depended on massive deceit—feints, false moves, concealment, and trickery. With Churchill's prodding, playing tricks on the high command of the Wehrmacht became a favorite sport for the Allied strategists. *Pupies! Pupies!* The Nazi officers screamed in rage and frustration in that memorable scene in *The Longest Day*, when they finally discovered the D-day feint of thousands of little paratrooper dolls dropped from the sky.

If the movements of vast armies can benefit from paradox, irony, and blasphemy in their supreme commanders, from deceit and trickery in strategy, why not the building of cities? Why not include the contributions that architects make to the building of cities? This question is worth asking because honesty has such a blemished track record in architecture. Like hope, it sounds good but it just doesn't work out in practice.

The ideal of honesty was the engine that launched architecture's modern movement. It was bequeathed to the modernists from their antecedents in the English arts and crafts movement and its Teutonic progeny, the Deutsche Werkbund and the Wiener Werkstadt. The idea was a reaction against the widespread use of the emergent new technologies of the mid-nineteenth century to replicate and mass-produce ancient decorative arts for new products, including architecture. Gothic Revival telephones and neoclassical sewing machines seemed utterly ridiculous. Why not make products and buildings that express the new realities, the new technologies, and the hopes embedded in them? Why not celebrate the nature of the materials themselves?

As a slogan, "truth" had everything going for it. What designer of artifacts could not be stirred by the moral crusade to embody and ennoble the real nature of things—the temper of the times, the process of manufacture, the inherent qualities of the substances one crafts into objects?

Unfortunately, almost always, something seems to get in the way. Consider two of modern architecture's totemic icons, Mies van der Rohe's Seagram Building in New York and Le Corbusier's *Unité d'Habitation* in Marseilles. Seagram was intended as an unadorned representation of the structural and tectonic realities of the steel-frame skyscraper, but it ran into difficulties. American fire-safety codes require structural steel in buildings over one story to be covered with a thick layer of fireproof goo. Mies solved the problem by simply putting another layer of nonstructural steel over the goo: decoration expressing the polemic of non-decoration.

Le Corbusier's polemics ran into similar problems in Marseilles. One of his Five Points for Modern Architecture prescribed a verdant ground plane running continuously under buildings. He envisioned the mass of buildings hoisted up on *pilotis*, columns that taper gracefully like table legs. He did not envision modern buildings with fat ankles. At the *Unité*, Corb's engineers explained to him that the great weight of the concrete structure needed to be rigidly anchored into foundations, and that the stresses were greatest where the columns met the foundation. No matter, Le Corbusier decided to taper the famous *pilotis* inward at the bottom anyway—graceful, but opposite to the patterns of stress. The columns are weakest where they are working hardest, and their connections to massive foundations are concealed underground.

Seagram Building, Chicago,
Mies van der Rohe

Pilotis Unité d'Habitation, Marseilles,
Le Corbusier

The point here is not that these iconic buildings are flawed masterpieces because they are not "honest"—quite the contrary; it is that artifice and deception are and always have been central to the architectural endeavor. After all, Michelangelo's four columns that hold the dome of St. Peters, the very pillars of Christianity, are real marble only at the bottom, and skillfully painted plaster over crude bricks up where you can't get close to them. Great theater, not truth.

Something similar applies to the making of urban buildings intended to fit gracefully into their cityscapes. Architects intent on making contextual urban buildings, particularly when the context of the new buildings is old, run into problems of dogma versus artifice similar to those that Mies and Le Corbusier faced. This is true even when the dogma is all about the continuity of the city.

In the 1960s, a few people began to wake up to the fact that destroying European cities in the name of Modern Architecture was not such a good idea. A foundational tract in the movement to rescue European urban culture from the wrecking ball was Aldo Rossi's *Architecture of the City.*[2] Despite Diane Ghirardo's heroic attempt to translate the floridities of Italian prose, the English version is vague, and difficult. What does come through is the intensity of Rossi's love of cities as the repository of memory, and his distance from the great wave of antihistorical nihilism that swept through Italian schools of architecture in the 1960s.

That book, and the university pedagogy that Rossi was part of, helped reestablish the detailed examination of building typology as fundamental to urban studies. The idea was to anchor the continuity of the city, not in replicating the stylistic surfaces of the old, but in understanding the fundamental spatial and tectonic order of the city. Typological studies, contextualism, and the continuity of urban civilization became synonymous with each other. The modernist crusade to reveal the truth of the times at all cost encountered a counter-crusade to maintain the heritage of the European city and its New World offspring.

Building typologies—recurrent patterns of how the spaces of buildings are organized, how one gets in and out of them, how they receive daylight and provide shelter, how they are made, how they resist gravity—are worthy of historical research. The trouble with typological studies as a prescription for the continuity of the city is that the very things that generate building typology change all the time in a flourishing, living city, and they change inexorably.

Consider the following conditions that fundamentally shape buildings that did not exist when the historical fabric of most of the world's cities was built:

— Fire safety laws that require safe paths in two directions from everywhere in a building

— Parking automobiles in or under buildings

— Access to people in wheelchairs

— Daylight to all habitable rooms

— Public land ownership or large aggregations of capital that make building projects larger than city blocks

— Floor plates large enough to accommodate modern corporations and institutions

None of these considerations are just technical details; they all are fundamental to the shaping of buildings and cities. These inexorable facts present an architect with a choice, a choice many make without articulating, even to themselves, exactly what they are doing. Contextualism—that is, building sympathetically to an existing place—and fidelity to historical typologies are not the same; they are not even close. One wonders what Aldo Rossi the theorist thought of Aldo Rossi the architect.

The act of balancing contradictory truths involves untruths, artifice. Artifice is a subtle matter—not amenable to rules, formulae, or codes. Because it is outside the domain of rule, artifice can be done badly or done well. It involves taste, skill, intuition, a feel for things: mêtis, as it was called by ancient Greeks. Admittedly, this realm of architectural disingenuousness—making buildings that look at least a little like something they are not really—is dangerous territory. The architect must be brave enough to ski close to the abyss of the egregiously phony, and skillful enough not to fall off the edge. As Churchill well knew, it is a disaster when the fake appears to be fake.

The need for untruth also varies widely from place to place. Think of three kinds of urban places:

First, there are places that don't matter, even to the people who live in them. They are part of the interchangeable, nondescript urban dross that has spread around the world like a great malignancy. For an architect or an urbanist, building in the dross can be engaging in its own way. There are ways to build worthwhile fragments within it, even if what's around them is beyond redemption.

Second, there are places that function as reliquaries. Once upon a time they had thriving economies, political importance, or flourishing movements in the arts, but now they serve principally as the record of the way things once were. Venice, Prague, and Williamsburg come to mind. Tourism, scholarship, and historic preservation keep them intact. They are like museum treasures.

Most of this book, however, is about places of a third kind (not to be confused with buildings of the third kind, discussed elsewhere). These places have living, ever-changing economies and political cultures, but they inhabit the ground of precious history. American cities like Boston and San Francisco join the great capitals of Europe on the list of places of the third kind. It is these places where acts of deceit are a necessary part of an architect's tool kit. Architects cannot do their job in these cities without well-developed disingenuousness, their own guardian of lies. The exact form that disingenuousness takes depends on the place itself—that is the whole idea.

Rome and San Francisco figure prominently in this text. Both are places of the third kind, par excellence. Both are also continuous cities par excellence. Both cities wear their history as a weathered face wears the experience of a life. Rome's transformations are stretched over two and a half millennia; San Francisco's are packed into a century and a half. Both are functioning and ever-changing parts of the modern world, and both are tourist destinations.

Much of what my colleagues and I have built is in San Francisco, which, like Rome, is an especially vivid case of the collision between time and place. San Francisco is a nineteenth-century city, a quite beautiful one, that reinvents itself culturally and economically every few years. The essential form of the city was well established by 1860, but in 2018, it is hardly an ossified reliquary. It is a jumping place with a booming economy of innovation that is the envy of the world. It also has tensions and social problems, and, God knows, volumes of rules that its nineteenth-century builders could not have imagined.

Like most of the world's cities, it had a long and disastrous affair with the Ruptured City, lasting from immediately after WWII until the mid-1970s. Sooner than most, San Francisco aborted the affair and rediscovered itself. By the mid-1970s, public sentiment in San Francisco had turned violently against the Ruptured City and its manifestations in urban renewal, public housing, and freeway building. As recounted, the city's powerful redevelopment czar, Justin Herman, was literally strangled by an irate citizen. Since the last quarter of the twentieth century, contextualism has been a survival strategy for San Francisco architects—just as appearing to be a fascist or a communist were at their respective times of ascendancy in Rome. My own career is deeply entwined with San Francisco's special form of narcissism. For architects of my generation in San Francisco, the choices have been simple—design contextually or forget about building anything in the city.

As I have learned, there is more to building contextually than simply declaring the intention to do so. There are tricks involved—chicanery, secret ways of telling untruths. It is an unseen game with unspoken rules. The rules are not really rules, but the penalties for playing the game badly are severe. People scream at you, call you nasty names; neighborhood groups vilify you; newspapers denounce you; bureaucrats thwart you; clients fire you. It is no joke.

Like others whose careers lead them to be tricksters and liars, a contextual architect's skills benefit from years of practice—like professional card players, or magicians. Among my peers, most may not be willing to reveal their secrets. I, however, would not undertake writing this book if I did not have an incurable didactic streak. So here goes—a revelation of the secrets behind a project that achieves the miracle of being unobjectionable in a city that objects passionately to almost everything.

Zygmunt Arendt House / San Francisco
Photo ©Bruce Damonte

Zygmunt Arendt House is home to fifty formerly homeless seniors in the middle of NOPA, a handsome neighborhood of lovingly restored, mostly Victorian houses. The people who live in NOPA are not rich-rich but are sufficiently well-off to own or rent real estate in a nice part of the most expensive city in the nation. All of them without exception are partisans on behalf of the Continuous City. They invested in it, they live in it, and they love it like helicopter parents.

San Francisco has a modest program providing about 300 units a year of supportive housing for the homeless, making small dents in the city's trenchantly persistent population of about 6,600 poor souls living on the streets. The city policy is to give first priority for these precious units to those who have been homeless the longest, the hard-core chronic cases including the mentally ill and substance dependent.

When we first received this commission, we scheduled a meeting with the well-organized and highly vocal neighborhood group. To our surprise, these well-heeled neighbors had no problem with fifty wretched, long-term residents of doorways coming to live among them. What did raise their passionately articulated ire was the prospect of a new building in the neighborhood that looked anything like it housed fifty wretched, long-term residents of doorways. Our instructions were clear, because nothing gets built in San Francisco that is opposed by well-organized neighbors.

NOPA is on hilly terrain, and most of its buildings are San Francisco's famous "painted ladies"—twenty-five-foot-wide one- or two-family structures with bay windows, heavily encrusted with Victorian ornament that the builders of the day could buy at the lumber yard. This is the city built exactly as Anne Vernez-Moudon had described years ago.

I had decades of practice with these situations, but this was an extreme case. Hard-core homeless in a fancy neighborhood with a site and program for a structure six times bigger than the little buildings stepping with the slopes around it. For multiple reasons having to do with security, efficiency, handicapped access, fire safety, and cost, this had to be a building with an elevator and flat corridors. Third, the little studio apartments were half the width of the generous Victorian rooms that generated the neighborhood streetscape of rhythmic bay windows. Finally, the highly "empowered" (a word of the times) neighbors absolutely would not consider anything that they could label with the hated epithet "modern."

So began the game of deceit.

The analytic drawings that interested John Hedjuk thirty years before came in handy with this most difficult trick—making a big building with flat floors resonate with much smaller buildings that step with the slope. This is a compound trick with several parts, blurred together like the machinations of a crooked card dealer. By using a half-stop elevator for handicapped access, the floors do actually step half a level. On the downhill side, the top floor is cut away, creating a step, and a nice roof deck, where incurable smokers find refuge. Then there are lots of little manipulations of the heights of windowsills and tops, parapets, and push-pull in and out in plan to complete the illusion.

To approximate the dimensions of the historic bay windows all around, we gave each unit a half of a bay divided in the middle. On a tight budget one cannot truly replicate Victorian detail, but simple trims and cornices, deliberately a bit overscaled, give the facades a density of detail and play of shadow much like the Victorian neighbors.

So—tricks, tricks, tricks, and to what end?

This work is a reversal of conventional ideas about context and typology á la Rossi et al. Here the architecture is not an expression of the underlying type, but a concealment of it. There is sleight of hand involved in making the Continuous City when the conditions that produced the city are not continuous, but magic tricks or card tricks work only when they are invisible. In addition to these typological manipulations, there is no compunction here about archaicism in the details: ornamented cornices, overscaled robustness in the trim. Context trumps zeitgeist; dishonesty abounds; just what our modernist friends, still clinging to nineteenth-century ideas of historical integrity, consider the depths of moral turpitude.

Zygmunt Arendt House tenants /
San Francisco
Photo ©Bruce Damonte

The fifty homeless souls rescued from doorways, filth, and degradation are the precious truths of Zygmunt Arendt House. They all look pretty good now—cleaned up, nicely dressed, most with a noticeable air of serenity. Some are astonishingly articulate about their homeless years and the utter transformation they have experienced. Architecture is their guardian of lies.

Hunters View / San Francisco, as it was 1943–2012

Hunters View / San Francisco, as it is 2014–present
Photo ©Tim Griffith

CHAPTER 8
From Hope to Love

An architect is a foot soldier in the making of the world, and there is nothing as vivid as the foxhole view of events. For a long time, I have had this privileged vantage point, as America's policies for housing the poor shifted from Catherine Bauer's dashed dreams of a rationalist utopia to the ideals of the Continuous City. Henry Cisneros's appearance at the Congress for the New Urbanism in 1994 started a great chain of events that eventually created for me and many of my colleagues chances to rebuild some of the hellish places that trapped generations of American poor. While doing this work, we have gotten to know many of these people, heard their stories, and watched their lives transform with the rebuilding.

Three of our projects fit exactly into the chronology of chapter 2: Othello Station in Seattle, Hunters View in San Francisco, and Jordan Downs in Watts (Los Angeles). All were planned and built as emergency housing for war industries in the same year, 1943—respectively serving Boeing Aircraft, the Hunters Point Naval Shipyard, and Fontana Steel and Hughes Aircraft. Never before in history did an entire society mobilize at the scale and speed of America in WWII. It is the only time the United States has ever mounted a housing program on the scale of Amsterdam, Paris, Vienna, or Rome, but this massive investment of 1943, unlike its European brethren, was measured solely in numbers. Today there are no pilgrimages of international architecture students savoring the beauties of this residue of wartime expedience.

In all three cities, public housing authorities assumed ownership and management of the projects shortly after the war. In all three cities, there were additions and minor upgrades to the wartime housing in 1954, but these additions followed the original design ideas that had been established with the Wagner/Steagall Act in 1937. These "temporary" projects built on the cheap remained as public housing for the next fifty-five to sixty years, until the rebuilding that started twenty years ago and continues sporadically in small increments today.

At Hunters View and Jordon Downs, we started right at the beginning and have continued through all the steps of community engagement, master planning, entitlements, architectural design, and construction. Step one in these long journeys was getting to know the tenants, listening to their stories, and building some measure of trust with people in whom mistrust of anyone related to housing authorities or redevelopment was a natural reflex.

Hunters View was San Francisco's most violent and decrepit public housing project. Though it was partially vacant and boarded up, Hunters View remained home to about 200 mostly African American families, some of whom had lived there for three or four generations. As architects for the rebuilding, we had regular community meetings on the site, and we listened to an incredible litany of tragic stories of shootings, rape, roaches, rats, fatal fires, the wasted lives of young people, and gang terror so violent that kids could not venture into the adjacent project without fear of being shot.

At one community meeting, we walked around with small groups of residents and asked them to record what they thought about our initial proposals for various parts of the site. When the larger group reconvened, we asked a resident named James to report on his group's observations about the southern edge of the site.

James is a white man about thirty-five, who had lived in Hunters View since 1979. With no affectation whatsoever, James speaks in the cadences of his black neighbors, whom he refers to as his brothers and sisters. Each time I have seen him he has worn a huge Cleveland Cavaliers jersey down to his knees, behind which is a very substantial person. Most of the others on the tenants committee like it when James gets to collect the housing authority's fee for making dinner for the meeting, because his jambalaya is reputedly the best in the neighborhood. Initially James was reticent about doing the talking, but an aerial photograph that included the wreck of a community center just south of the site got him started. We didn't record his speech, but it went pretty much like this:

> "These young kids now with their guns—they don't even
> bother with drive-bys. They doing walk-bys: BAM! When we
> were growing up, it was different. Nobody got into trouble.
> We went to that community center, right there (pointing to
> the photograph) and it was clean and beautiful. I learned to
> shoot pool, I learned macramé [that's what he said] and
> I played basketball. We all did those things all the time.
> There was macramé stuff all over the neighborhood and
> nobody got in trouble. Now that place has fallen apart and the
> director is a bad man. He should go, and if you rebuilding
> this whole neighborhood, it don't make sense not to rebuild the
> community center."

I said to James that it would be hard to rebuild the community center, because it was not owned or operated by the housing authority that is sponsoring the rebuilding. I asked if it would be just as good to have new places for pool, macramé, and basketball on the Hunters View site instead of next door.

> *"NO!" he said, "you don't understand what I'm saying. The*
> *reason we didn't get in trouble was that kids from all over the*
> *hill went to the community center. I grew up with people from*
> *the other side of the hill. Some of them still my brothers and*
> *sisters. Now, Hunters View kids shoot people from the other*
> *side of the hill."*

There it was, clear as could be. James is a northern white man who excels at jambalaya. He is a San Franciscan who wears the colors of the Cleveland Cavaliers. He is a big, tough guy who is proud of the macramé he once made. And he considers black people who live on the other side of the hill his family. Compared to the teenage gunslingers of Hunters View, James has had a cosmopolitan, peaceful life.

I can't help thinking that there must be people like James in Gaza, Hebron, Sarajevo, Baghdad, and Aleppo—people whose life experience is as liberal and tolerant as his, and who have watched their communities fold in on themselves. Folding in is the trigger for the gratuitous violence that has made Hunters View a hellhole. In a much bigger and more dangerous way, it is the same folding in that is occurring many places in the world and has occurred many times in the past.

With James's moving speech, one sees the link to what one can do as an architect. First, focus the rebuilding as much on the linkages of Hunters View to the world outside as on replacing the squalid, horrible buildings. Second, embrace the principles of architecture and urbanism that give San Francisco's neighborhoods their distinctive charm and make the city such a desirable place to live; make Hunters View a part of the Continuous City. Third, and also important, is to embrace the optimism of the modern without its destructiveness; make the place new, bright, and clean—washed in sunlight, like Catherine Bauer and her revolutionary chums wanted, but without their terrible mistakes.

For a long time it has been wildly unfashionable to claim that architecture can help society. We suffer a generational embarrassment about the naive and hubristic claims of an earlier generation of architects and urbanists, the City of Hope crowd, who turned out to be so wrong. But James's story about how the physical isolation of Hunters View bred its culture of violence shows how the physical city shapes the psyche. You can't convince someone who has lived their life in Hunters View that architecture and urban design are not important.

We were well acquainted with the isolation/violence equation at Hunters View before meeting James. The only way in or out of Hunters View was a single straight street called Middle Point Drive that had views of the city. As soon as one stepped just a few feet off Middle Point, all sense of the city disappeared and one was in a terrifying, unshaped, unowned, unloved maze of incoherent squalor. In that maze we had our first well-attended community meeting, presided over by an articulate African American woman tenant with a polite, handsome seventeen-year-old son. The strong message of that first meeting was that the tenant group would fiercely resist any rebuilding plan that displaced people to other public housing sites during the reconstruction. Other projects had other gangs, and there was no way that Hunters View kids, boys especially, could survive in other projects.

Before the second community meeting two weeks later, we were told that the chair of the tenants committee had resigned because her son had been shot. He returned from the hospital and was sitting in front of their apartment, paralyzed in a wheelchair, when his assailants returned to finish the job, killing him. We realized that we had entered a world in our own city, but disconnected from it, that was totally outside our own experience or understanding.

As we worked on the plan and then the first buildings for Hunters View, we hired residents to work in our office to help them acquire some workforce skills. Their endless stories of mayhem, tragedy, and hopeless isolation helped prepare us for a next assignment, as we tried to prepare them for their next steps.

Grape Street Crips, Jordan Downs

Our next public housing reconstruction was the notorious Jordan Downs in Watts, home to Los Angeles's near-mythological street gang, the Grape Street Crips. Jordan Downs is three times the size of Hunters View, and when we started it was even more violent. It is 797 fully occupied units on eighty acres, with twenty acres of vacant land that would help accommodate phased reconstruction with no displacement to other sites. In 2009, the year we started, there were thirteen killings on the site. *Imagine that*: 2,000 or so people with thirteen murders in one year on the same isolated superblock. Through the efforts of the housing authority, social workers, and the LAPD, the level of violence abated by the time reconstruction began in 2017.

If unreconstructed Hunters View looked like a crumbling military base, unreconstructed Jordan Downs looked like a very large, well-maintained medium-security detention facility. Behind chain-link fences topped with razor wire were row upon row of identical two-story buildings, each distinguished from the others only by a huge black three-digit number. All of the ground-floor windows and many of the upper ones were encrusted with ad hoc layers of bars, razor wire, and expanded metal. As is typical of this generation of Ruptured City public housing, the land between the buildings was an amorphous maze of scattered parking lots, clotheslines, and ratty places for children to play.

When we prepared the plan for razing Jordon Downs and replacing it in phases with a beautiful Continuous City neighborhood, we had to shepherd the plan through the long process of an Environmental Impact Report (EIR). A California EIR includes a section on impacts on historic resources that must be prepared by acknowledged architectural historians. When we saw the first draft of this report, the historians claimed that Jordan Downs should not be touched because it was the country's largest fully intact example of New Deal housing policy.

I went through the roof.

Only the good sense of our clients and my partners prevented me from trumpeting an op ed saying that if Jordan Downs was a cultural artifact, the artifact had to include all the razor wire, bars, and gratings the tenants had installed for their survival; that if Jordan Downs was a cultural artifact worthy of preservation, it was so in the same sense as the landmarked Charleston Slave Market, but the slave market had not been preserved in its original use. Fortunately, cooler heads prevailed all round, and eventually the historians quietly agreed to approve the demolition. They had been right, though, that Jordan Downs was a powerful testament to New Deal housing policy and to its utter failure—exactly why its demolition was so imperative.

In the course of these conversations, it turned out that many of the residents did cherish one item they thought worthy of preservation—a scroungy tree in the middle of the site that they referred to as the Freedom Tree. There were two explanations for the significance of this tree and its name. The first was that it was the site of regular ceremonies when Jordan Downs residents were released from jail. For young men raised at Jordan Downs, jail was a rite of passage that almost all of them experienced, and celebration at the tree was part of the rite. The second explanation for the name was that if anyone was running for safety, the police would never dare go east or south of the Freedom Tree, because it was too dangerous for them. Make it to the tree and you were safe. As of this writing, the reconstruction is finally starting, and, sadly, the cherished Freedom Tree succumbed to old age and drought some time ago.

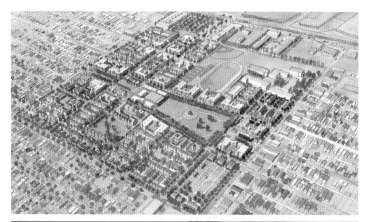

The community meetings at Hunters View and Jordan Downs left deep impressions—indelible faces, voices, and stories so different from my own. Perhaps the most memorable meeting was the third in the series of community meetings for the overall master plan of the Jordan Downs replacement. Something curious had occurred at the first two meetings, and the third meeting was conceived to address the problem. Jordan Downs and the Watts community around it grew exponentially during WWII as hundreds of thousands of African Americans were drawn, largely from the rural South, to employment in Los Angeles's burgeoning

Jordan Downs / Watts, Los Angeles; reconstruction master plan (above); reconstruction under construction (below)

war industries. For a long time after the war it remained an almost all-black community, even as the industries and the prosperity they brought disappeared.

Then, bit by bit, the population changed. Middle-class blacks moved away and were replaced in the project and the larger neighborhood with newcomers from Mexico and Central America. By 2009, when we started work on Jordon Downs, the project and the neighborhood were one-third African American and two-thirds Latino. But at the first two community meetings, the attendance was virtually all black—not a good political portent.

There were several explanations for the Latino boycott. Latino families often had far more people living in their units than were listed on the lease, and many had doubtful documentation. There was a widespread sense that participation in the planning process would trigger investigations of immigration status. Also there was fear of violence—that if Latinos participated there would be reprisals against them from black neighbors who did not want to relinquish the control they historically had over what happens in Watts.

The idea for getting the whole community on the same page at the third meeting was to load the agenda with irresistible political star power, including Los Angeles's young, ambitious, and super-polished Latino mayor, Antonio Villaraigosa; and Watts's own Washington powerhouse, Congresswoman Maxine Waters, chair of the Congressional Black Caucus. What a lineup!

Well, it worked. The big gym that functioned as a meeting room was totally packed—black and brown about equally, and once the ice was broken with this meeting, it remained packed and racially mixed for every subsequent meeting. Mayor Villaraigosa and Congresswoman Waters on the same stage was a picture of local history. The audience may have been mostly Latino, but the normally suave and articulate mayor acted like a somewhat nervous and tentative guest on what was clearly Maxine Water's home turf. So go the politics in that part of LA.

Over the course of the three meetings I had gotten to know one of the more talkative and articulate tenants, who went by the name Scorpio Smith. He was good-looking guy, with well-tended cornrows, and a physiognomy that was the product of a lot of time in a weight room somewhere. After the mayor/congresswoman meeting, Score (as people called him) asked me if I wanted to take a walk with him and see Jordan Downs the way the housing authority had not shown me. I immediately changed my plane reservation back to San Francisco so I could spend the next couple of hours with him.

As we walked I heard his story, or the parts he wanted to tell me. He was forty-four years old and had grown up in Jordan Downs, and his weight room was series of prison yards where he had spent much of his life. Neither that afternoon nor subsequently did I ever ask what his offenses were, and he never told me, other than to say that he had been a gangbanger and by the age of fourteen he, like his peers, was "banging hard." He currently lived an hour away in the mostly white community of Seal Beach with his white girlfriend, Jan. She had been a kindergarten teacher in fancy Newport Beach, but at the time of the 1992 Rodney King riots in South Central Los Angeles, she decided there were more important things to do with her life, and she moved to Watts. She and Scorpio had been together for some time and had established something called Parolees for Change. It was an accredited tutoring program that allowed kids not permitted in public school because they had felony records to earn a high school diploma. It was a hand-to-mouth operation scraping by on small grants, but apparently they had rescued quite a number of lost kids. Impressive people.

Scorpio showed me a series of unseen boundaries winding through the Jordan Downs superblock, denoting black gang turf, Latino gang turf, and demilitarized zones. The only real economy was the drug trade, and drug politics were like regular politics in Watts, with the now-minority blacks clinging fiercely to power.

There was a several-year interval between completing the Jordan Downs reconstruction master plan and finally being hired to design buildings for the first construction phases. There were revisions and refinements of the plan, and we needed to hold another community meeting in 2016. So much time had passed in the many steps through bureaucracies and funding sources that I was surprised at how warmly we were received and how many familiar faces there were. Familiar faces eager for the change finally to happen, but no Scorpio.

I asked the housing authority guy in charge of community relations what had become of him. He hesitated for a moment before telling me that Scorpio had been—uh, "reincarcerated." Oh shit. My heart sank.

Subsequently I heard that the reincarceration was a parole technicality. He had been released and had finally found a good job as an electrician, a trade he had learned in prison. But on his first day on this coveted job, his employer terminated him because, as a multiple felon, he rendered the employer uninsurable. What a brutally stacked deck Scorpio was playing against, as he had all his life. As of this writing, this highly likable casualty of "the country's largest fully intact example of New Deal housing policy" appears finally to be on his feet after a long and terrible journey.

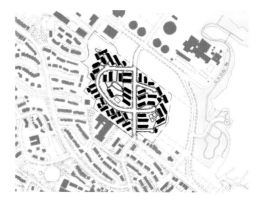

Hunters View figure/ground plan, as it was

Hunters View master plan

Hunters View partially constructed
Photo ©Steve Proehl

Above and below: Hunters View, San Francisco
Photos ©Tim Griffith

Above and below: Hunters View, San Francisco. Mithun/Solomon Architects and GLS Landscape Architects
Photos ©Tim Griffith

CHAPTER 9
Hybrid 1: Carl Mackley Houses

When I began to think about the Continuous City and the Ruptured City, the City of Love and the City of Hope, I saw it as an unambiguous matter.

There has been a long struggle between two streams of thought that are clearly different from one another, and history has made a clear decision about who was right and who was wrong. There were bad guys who did harm, and good guys who did good. Like everyone else of my generation, I was tempted to be a bad guy in my youth because everybody else was doing it, but I can congratulate myself (as I do throughout this book) on the decision to live my life as a good guy doing good. It was easy to see that bad guys built slab blocks with buildings lined up in rows, and good guys built perimeter blocks with buildings bending around corners and defining streets. As it turns out, the real story, like most true stories, is more complicated, nuanced, and interesting. Sometimes cross-breeding (of ideas, plants, animals, or humans) produces offspring with a special ambiguous charm.

Hybrid 1: Carl Mackley Houses

To show that cross-breeding has gone on for a long time, this story dates from the mid-1930s and is brushed by the then-youthful Catherine Bauer, the iconic figure who appears prominently in our story. When Bauer headed off on her fun-filled European journeys of 1930 and 1932 she was given lists of contacts by her dear friends Lewis Mumford and Philadelphia architect Oskar Stonorov.

Both Mumford and Stonorov had their own agendas in helping her plan her travels. They guessed correctly that the impressionable, idealistic, wildly energetic, and resourceful young Catherine would come home as a passionate importer of the latest in European social housing policy and design thinking. They also guessed correctly that charming, adventurous, and amusing young Catherine would find a warm welcome among their European friends. Very warm, as it turned out.

Her trips bore abundant fruit. The 1930 itinerary included a three-day seminar at Frankfurt am Main led by city architect Ernst May, author of a series of radical, beautifully executed new housing estates on ex-urban sites around the city. May was a most refined and prolific designer of a new type of housing and urban development known as the Zeilenbau, consisting of parallel rows of low-rise apartments oriented to maximize exposure of each unit to the sun. The Frankfurt

Zeilenbau in its pure form

projects, especially one called Romerstadt, were a revelation to Catherine Bauer, both aesthetically and in their social program. For better and for worse, that three-day seminar would have echoes in American public housing for more than fifty years.

The trip provided the material for a prize-winning essay in *Fortune* magazine on European housing and laid the groundwork for her magisterial book *Modern Housing* in 1935. The *Fortune* essay also opened the door for her to contribute to the New York Museum of Modern Art's book *America Can't Have Housing* that accompanied a major housing exhibition in 1934.

Except for projects intended to illustrate bad practice, there was very little American work included in the MoMA show. An exception was Oskar Stonorov's Carl Mackley Houses, designed for the Philadelphia Hosiery Workers Union, with Bauer's participation. Stonorov's design as it was shown at MoMA could easily have been done by Ernst May or Walter Gropius—a strictly conventional (according to the new convention) Zeilenbau—three immaculately white parallel apartment slabs, every apartment facing the sun with the same orientation, like morning glories.

Oskar Stonorov's Carl Mackley Houses as exhibited at MoMA

Karl Mackley Houses was built, became a landmark in American social housing, has been loved and respected for eighty years, and has recently been restored. Though it is almost always credited to Oskar Stonarov, it was not Stonarov's design that was built. Stonorov's much less famous partner, Alfred Kastner, executed the project and changed the design fundamentally. Stonorov's design was conceived for MoMA's audience; Kastner's was done in concert with the future residents from the Hosiery Workers Union.

Kastner's design has four rows of apartments, not three, and they are not simple unidirectional bars. Where each of his bars meets the street, it turns and there is an additional stack of units, so that the wide-open spaces between the bars are partially enclosed by a semicontinuous street wall. The middle of each bar is inflected inward, so that the shapeless void between the bars in Stonorov's scheme becomes a series of semidefined courtyards. These small variations make

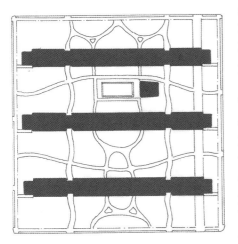

Stonorov's design

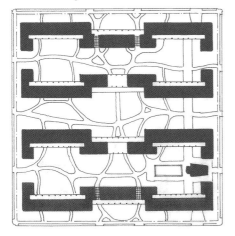

Alfred Kastner's design

a huge difference. The beloved and enduring Karl Mackley design is a half-breed—half cowboy, half Indian, a melding of two typologies: the courtyard perimeter block and the unidirectional slab block.

The principal thinkers about American housing design at the time of the New Deal—led by Bauer, Mumford, and Stonorov—thought it was impossible to build decent modern housing within the fabric of American cities, that American street grids and patterns of land ownership would not permit it. They accepted the European idea that egalitarian access to sunlight was a predicating condition for an egalitarian society. The unidirectional slab block, the Zeilenbau, was a conceptual breakthrough that achieved equal distribution of sunlight but demanded large, unencumbered sites such as Romerstadt. It demanded that poor people move to isolated locations so they could live, not as part of a city but in an architectural dream of a better world to come.

We know now the disaster that idea produced, but Carl Mackley Houses avoided that fate.

Aerial photographs taken when the project was new show that, as Stonorov wanted, Carl Mackley was built on vacant land, far from anything. The photographs also show that the surrounding land was subdivided with a grid of streets that would eventually fill in with new houses. Because the project has the continuous street frontages of a perimeter block, and because it was built of Philadelphia's common, long-lasting brick, the project has simply blended into the neighborhood that grew up around it. The residents, citizens of the Continuous City, never suffered the stigma of "project dwellers."

Stonorov designed Carl Mackley for an isolated place in classic Ruptured City style for MoMA and its audience. It now has an honored place on the National Register of Historic Places, thanks to the subtle, nondoctrinaire design of Alfred Kastner, not to the ringing polemics of Stonorov or his powerhouse protégé. Still, it is the Stonorov sculpture of Catherine Bauer that stands in the lobby of HUD, and Alfred Kastner is a name known only to a very few housing geeks.

Beijing street life

CHAPTER 10
Hybrid 2: The Chinese Puzzle

It is hard to conceive that the fiercest revolutionaries in the Western world—the likes of Robespierre, Bakunin, Marinetti, or Lenin—ever in their wildest imaginings really thought that their ideas would make their homeland look entirely different within the space of a couple of decades. After the revolutions, France still looked pretty much like France, and Russia looked like Russia. Italian futurists, for all their rant, would have been horrified if they had brought about an Italy that no longer looked like Italy.

China is one place where the force of an idea completely changed the face of the largest cities and the whole of the urban landscape in little more than twenty years. The idea that brought about the change was not the monumental social transformation that propelled Mao's revolution. The change was really a technocrat's change, one with intentions more narrowly pragmatic than grandly ideological. Think of the world turned upside down by a zoning ordinance.

It is the same idea that we have encountered over and over in the pages of this book—not an idea that fully originated in China, but one that found resonance and reinforcement in ancient Chinese custom.

If you go through the northern Chinese countryside by train, you pass village after village with basically the same layout, whether they appear ancient or recent. A long-standing convention of planning and construction is clearly at work. There are parallel rows of one-story buildings all oriented in the same direction, with occasional cross bars defining the spaces between buildings as courtyards, and when there are no cross bars, the buildings define little streets. Whatever the topography or natural features of the land, all the main buildings run east–west and dwellings always have a main space facing south, usually to a courtyard.

This rural village pattern translated to urban scale and density became the old, now almost completely eradicated, hutong fabric of Beijing, the term "hutong" referring to the little lanes that ran between the one-story courtyard complexes. For centuries, the hutongs of Beijing were the armature for an incredibly rich social and mercantile life, a unique and self-sustaining form of urban grace. In the few bits of hutong fabric that remain, one can feel the intimately interconnected way of life the hutongs nurtured—intricate networks of courtyards and lanes for children, for the elderly, for merchants and artisans, for an entire urban population.

Beijing hutong, remnants

The book *The Last Days of Old Beijing*,[1] by Michael Meyer, an American English teacher who chose to live in an intact hutong in the last years before its demolition, is the heart-rending account of what happened to the people he knew in the hutong, as they were forcibly dispersed to life in the new China. For the dumpling maker, the cell phone repair whiz, the lonely widow across the courtyard, and many others he knew intimately, their entire sustaining social network and source of identity were eradicated. Meyer's fine narrative brings each of these personal tragedies vividly to life. It is truly painful reading, the bitter human side of the transformation from Continuous City to Ruptured City.

A very big thing had happened: the urban population in Chinese cities exploded as war and civil war ravaged the peasant economies of the countryside in the 1930s and 1940s. After 1949, Beijing's courtyard houses that had provided gracious living for a single middle-class family were expropriated as dwellings for eight or nine families, mostly rural immigrants. In the following decades, courtyards were stuffed with ad hoc structures, and the primitive infrastructure of communal latrines and bathhouses was overwhelmed by the manyfold increase in population. By the late 1980s, half of Beijing, some 7.5 million people, were living at a density of three square meters or less per person in dwellings without heating or plumbing. The darkest days of Dickensian London or the Lower East Side of New York as photographed by Jacob Reis never approached this level of overcrowding.

In the early 1990s, as China began its rise from poverty, its planners and bureaucrats faced a choice between two sharply different paths to redressing the most massive housing crises the world had ever seen. The two choices were the same contending ideas that battle their way through Western urban history all through the pages of this book: the Continuous City and the Ruptured City.

The Ruptured City choice was a ready-made amalgam of the ancient Chinese practice one observes in countless villages, combined with the Western idea of the Zeilenbau. Chinese planners discovered the diagrams of parallel bars of buildings separated by the reach of a winter shadow that Walter Gropius and his students had produced at the Bauhaus and later at Harvard. These were the same diagrams that so captivated Catherine Bauer that she made them a centerpiece of her seminal book *Modern Housing*.

Chinese planners saw in these diagrams the ancient pattern of Chinese villages translated to the scale and density that could address China's stupendous housing need. They had to make only two small adjustments. First was to rotate the diagrams ninety degrees to recreate the honorific south-facing main rooms that Chinese consider axiomatic. Second was to create legislation mandating the pattern universally for new housing. It became law that all dwellings have southern exposure and that the dimensions between buildings relate to the azimuth of the winter sun in each municipality—very specific numbers. In the northern cities including Beijing and Tianjin, the gap between buildings could be neither less nor more than 1.6 times their height—not more because density was so needed, and not less so that every dwelling would receive at least two hours of direct sunlight all winter.

What the application of the Zeilenbau-based legislation did not consider was that the change of scale, from 1.6 times one story to 1.6 times six stories or more, fundamentally changed the nature and the use of urban space. The intimate, life-nurturing lanes and courtyards of old Beijing disappeared completely, replaced by vast, vacant no-man's lands of the sort that doomed the Parisian *Grand Ensemble* and the worst of American public housing. Same ideas, same rationale, same pattern, same cultural disaster; only far, far bigger. The dumpling maker, the cell phone

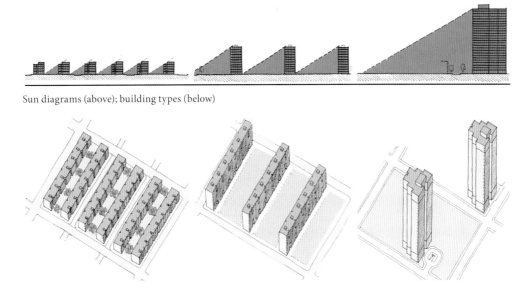

Sun diagrams (above); building types (below)

repair whiz, the laughing children, and the lonely widow had nowhere to go. Under the pressure of furious growth, a complex, centuries-old human ecology simply vanished.

Even if one were to decide that daylight in dwellings was the only criterion by which to judge the qualities of a city, the Chinese prescriptions—for universal south orientation, two hours of direct winter sun, and building separations 1.6 times the height of buildings—are impossibly crude and reductive measures for a complex and subtle phenomenon. We can observe cities (like Rome) that have pervasively beautiful light indoors and in the streets to see that daylight is a complex matter that concerns issues of contrast, glare, reflectivity, balance, and color; and certainly part of the poetics of daylight is variation and difference. The Chinese system is reduction upon reduction: daylight as the only criterion, and daylight is prescribed by the crudest oversimplification.

In the big cities of China, particularly northern cities, a new urban landscape of row upon row of midrise flats, or in many places row upon row of identical high-rises, stretches in all directions to the horizon, except the horizon itself is rarely visible in the miasma of brown murk that passes for air. The Chinese adopted the slab-block model of the open superblock or Zeilenbau far more rigidly and massively than its European originators or its American enthusiasts. Nowhere on earth have the ideas of the City of Hope been executed more massively or with more fervor than

The New China

in China. The Chinese program to rehouse hundreds of millions of people is the largest and most rapid construction enterprise ever attempted. All the social housing programs for the whole of the twentieth century in Europe and the United States combined add up to a small fraction of what China achieved in twenty years beginning in the early 1990s. The product of that generation of fierce activity is immediately obvious to visitors to almost any Chinese city.

About the time this rigid convention of superblocks—parallel rows of housing with utter desolation between—was being established, China was offered an alternative by its most revered architect, urbanist, and teacher, Professor Wu Liangyong of Tshingua University in Beijing. Working with a small group of students, Professor Wu designed and built a prototype for dense new courtyard housing that retained the spatial magic and the nurturing social armature of the ancient city. Their Ju'er Hutong is by every measure the Continuous City, just as its rival pattern is the embodiment of the Ruptured City as it was realized in the West.[2]

As an urban pattern and in its architectural detail, the Ju'er Hutong married the demographic realities of modern China to the ancient charm of Beijing. Comfortable, modern apartments, all with the requisite south light, surround an intimate network of communal courtyards with connecting passages through and under buildings. The fine hand of a modern architect versed in historic Chinese vernacular appears in the details of eaves, doorways, and rooftops, not as Chinatown kitsch but as embellishment to a gracious living environment.

The Ju'er Hutong was designed and published as a widely distributed book with Professor Wu's prestige behind it; then it was built, well covered in the architectural press around the world, and feted with many honors. Then it was ignored completely as China moved forward with its colossal housing program.

Ju'er Hutong

As one experiences the now slightly tattered, idiosyncratic charm of the Ju'er Hutong, it is not hard to see why it was rejected as a model. Thought, skill, imagination, scholarship, time, and talent are qualities not easily translated to the scale of the challenge—rehousing many hundreds of millions of people in a few years. Chinese bureaucracies are not peopled with thousands of Professor Wus (although, as we have learned, there are a few).

Plus there is another insidious factor that doomed Professor Wu's lovely prototype. This may seem like a technical detail, but it is actually a big deal. Architects in China are paid a tiny fee for designing a building—a fee too small even to cover the cost of producing a set of drawings. This does not apply to prestige commissions such as concert halls or museums, but it affects most of the normal buildings that constitute the urban fabric. The way that architects and engineers who design housing make a living is through reuse fees that are normally equal to the original fee for each reuse. If a developer builds a housing estate of one hundred identical buildings, the architect receives one hundred times his original fee. That is a partial explanation for the ubiquitous model of giant superblocks with identical buildings. This fee structure applies to luxury buildings as well as worker's housing. In the vast sprawl-scapes of Shanghai, Beijing, and Tianjin/Binhai it is quite normal to see a skillfully designed and handsomely built thirty-story apartment building repeated a hundred times in a giant gated superblock.

Other factors, too, have contributed to the Ruptured City formula that has governed Chinese housing for twenty-five years. Micro-municipalities do not collect property tax. They pay for their municipal services by leasing land for development, and the micro-municipalities compete ruthlessly with one another to attract these leases. Developers shop around, and they build wherever they can get the best deal. This quirk of tax policy helps explain the widely scattered, totally disconnected huge development projects in the bizarre landscapes of the new economic development zones: the very antithesis of the Continuous City.

While the formula that has governed twenty-five years of the Chinese housing explosion is simple and easy to understand, the urban culture this formula has eradicated was complex, elusive to describe, and not so easily reducible. The formula goes like this: First, there is a giant grid of huge, widely spaced arterial roads, six or sometimes eight lanes wide—impossible to walk along and hell on a bicycle. Scattered randomly about within this grid are gated development superblocks, usually consisting of hundreds of copies of the same building, aligned in rows so that all apartments face south. The vacant and desolate spaces between buildings, with exactly prescribed dimensions, are usually "landscaped" but are devoid of life; you hardly see anyone.

Hundreds of millions of dwellings are built to this dystopian Ruptured City formula. Surely this is the world's greatest testament to the disaster of reductive thinking, of simplistic mechanization of complex phenomena. It represents an epistemological lobotomy of half the human mind that major thinkers from Oswald Spencer to Martin Heidegger, from Lewis Mumford to Christian Norburg-Shulz, have railed against. More about this in the section called "Part III, Ideas."

Bleak New China: "courtyard" (above); streetscape (below)

Hexie (pronounced huh-shay)

Perhaps it was the height of hubris on my part to think of this dilemma as a solvable problem, to think that one could take on the ruthless pragmatism and intransigent rigidities of Chinese housing practice—the 1.6 gaps, the two hours of winter sunlight, the single set of simple drawings producing tens of thousands of units. Could we take on all that and still recapture the human soul of Chinese cities—the throbbing street life, the tiny courts, playing children, old men at mah jong, the neighborhood dumpling makers, and all the rest? Is it possible to build a technocratic city for millions and for that city to have a soul, a Chinese soul?

We have had a go at it.

The story has complex beginnings that included (1) my immersion in Chinese housing practice in all its rigid, universalizing, simple-minded craziness, (2) horror at what was being produced mile after mile at incredible speed to newly house hundreds of millions, and (3) a network of well-connected consultants and bureaucrats in the booming city of Tianjin who had been my UC Berkeley students. This group included a distinguished planner named Huo Bin, who did a postdoc at Berkeley and had been one of Professor Wu Liangyong's last doctoral students. Huo Bin is a well-traveled and well-read cosmopolitan urbanist, and he was planning director for a vast new port and industrial development zone called Binhai, adjacent to Tianjin.

Through my Berkeley network, I was invited to give a series of lectures at Tianjin University and to Tianjin planning bureaucrats about my impressions of new Chinese housing, and to compare it to American and European social housing. I did not let my spotty knowledge deter me, and I gave these lectures my full-throated opinions. What's to lose, I thought?

Some months later, to my astonishment, I heard from Huo Bin indirectly that he would like me to lead the planning of a major new project—tens of thousands of housing units in Binhai as a critical counterplan to business as usual. Wow!

Undertaking this incredible challenge depended on trust and friendship with an extraordinary colleague, Leon Huang, who after his student years at Berkeley moved to Tianjin from Shanghai and established one of the most successful urban design practices in China—a brilliant designer, a fiercely hard worker, a truly good guy, and also a politically savvy actor.

After an exchange of correspondence, maps, zoning rules, and the like, we arranged a trip to Tianjin to finalize a contract, see the site, and begin work. The trip from Tianjin out to its new satellite Binhai was mind boggling—imagine a place half the size of Los Angeles, all under construction at the same time, with widely dispersed construction sites for huge projects, none of which had any apparent relationship or connection to one another. When we arrived at our site after a long, long drive, my mouth dropped. This was, hands down, without question, the uncontestably ugliest segment of planet Earth I had ever seen. I had never imagined such a place.

It was dead flat and completely empty, not a building or tree or anything as far as the eye could see in every direction. Of course, the eye could not see very far because the middle landscape disappeared into a dense reddish-brown haze that made midday in summer seem like twilight on Mars. The Google Earth views of the site had shown the ground as pitch black, which we thought was a quirk of early Google Earth satellite photography. No quirk. Most of the ground for miles around was pitch black, since the site and its neighbors had been used for years as a storage and distribution area for coal. Miles and miles of coal, and coal dust was one component of the haze. I don't know what the red part was. Incredible.

Our site, Hexie New City

"Well, here we are," one of our hosts said cheerily: the site for Hexie (Harmony) New City, the project that would fulfill all of our dreams for a bright new kind of humane and lively Chinese community.

One further thing the tour leader explained: Although one had no sense of it, we were standing only about five kilometers from the sea, at the high point of the Hexie site—a little less than two meters above sea level. Drainage was, to put it mildly, an issue. We had already seen on visits to

Tianjin how during and after an ordinary moderate rain, storm drains erupted and the entire center of the city flooded—cars floated and people took pushing their bicycles through meter deep water as a normal hazard of a morning commute. Hexie had the same issue in spades.

After the somewhat shattering site visit, we met with Huo Bin, who briefed us on the project and explained what he hoped we could do. He said that Hexie New City was under special dispensation as an innovative, experimental project with foreign consultants. Some deviation from standard practice would be tolerated by the technocrats he operated under, but as he explained further, it appeared that the deviations were very limited. Most sacrosanct was the rule for two hours of direct southern sunlight for every unit all winter. While that did not absolutely mandate the deadly parallel rows of buildings 1.6 times their height apart, no one had ever found another way to do it that did not lose density. Losing density from the standard pattern was strictly forbidden. The tyranny of numbers is absolute; no question about it.

This new housing was to be for young industrial workers in the Binhai Economic Development Zone, many of them rural refugees with their first residence permits. A residence permit is the first step up the Chinese economic ladder from the status of homeless squatter. Many of the dwellings would therefore be subsidized low-income units and could not be more expensive to design and produce than the ubiquitous cookie-cutter rows of identical flats that one sees everywhere in China.

What an assignment!

Not everything was totally bleak, as Huo Bin further explained. The site, which appeared to be the very epicenter of nowhere, was actually at the nexus of an elaborate new public transportation infrastructure—light rail, subways, and commuter trains—connecting to nearby job centers, some of it already under construction. Creating a development pattern that did not load the hopelessly congested roads with more traffic and took advantage of the new public transportation would be viewed very favorably.

So we went to work, I with a small team in my office and Leon Huang with assistants in Tianjin. Over several months the master plan evolved as the combination of some simple ideas and one very complex idea. The simple ideas were these:

—The first was a grand move to establish a sense of place in the boundless, featureless landscape. The initial transportation infrastructure, a bus rapid transit, had been projected to run right through the middle of the site. We embraced this idea, splitting the two directions of a transit boulevard around a huge crescent-shaped park, Hexie's Central Park: identity for the place at the very beginning.

—The big park was also the much-needed flood control strategy, serving as a giant detention pond. All the streets would slope gently toward the park, which would slowly decant storm water to an unpolluted stream to the sea.

— We met with Huo Bin's transportation planners, who told us that since much of the transportation infrastructure was at an early stage of design, we could recommend locations for subway stations and bus stops that best served our new district. We chose locations at the perimeter of our site that allowed us to create a giant Y shape of pedestrian/bicycle streets that would be the commercial high street of each neighborhood and provide places for the profusion of small merchants, services, and micro-entrepreneurs that seem to erupt spontaneously in Chinese cities when the conditions permit. We were well aware that this "spontaneous" mercantile life would need a sophisticated program of recruiting, leasing, management, and subsidy to really work, so that was part of the plan. The pedestrian/bicycle streets would also be the location of neighborhood centers in each subdistrict, providing day care, clinics, and social services.

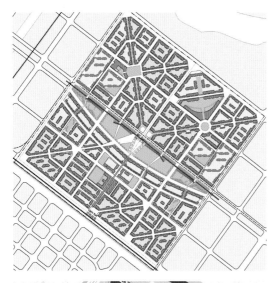

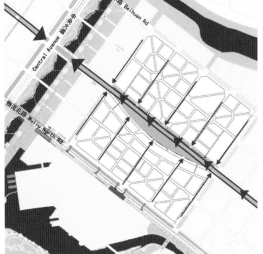

Hexie New City master plan (above);
Hydrology diagram (below)

The final big idea for the master plan is more subtle and complex. It consisted of three parts: (1) finding a means of conforming to the unalterable rule for two hours of direct winter sun for every apartment, (2) providing the requisite housing density, and (3) somehow re-creating the complex and intimate networks of lanes and courtyards that for centuries had nurtured the precious human ecology of urban China that had vanished altogether in the furious housing boom of the last decades.

We puzzled over this problem for weeks and finally discovered that patterns of buildings and small city blocks that varied in height and building configuration could achieve all three goals simultaneously: density, sunlight for all, and rich networks of intimate lanes, alleys, and courts. Admittedly, this required far more complex and varied buildings than the standard rows of identical cookie-cutter flats. Simplifying and standardizing, dealing with design cost and production cost, were beyond the scope, schedule, and fee for the master plan, so at that point we simply prepared a handsome presentation of the master plan ideas and the thinking behind them, for Huo Bin to share with other officials and decision makers.

We have no clue what actually transpires in Chinese bureaucracies, but after some months, we received word that our master plan had been well received, and we were being hired to take the next step, a much more detailed plan for a large segment of the plan—a demonstration neighborhood. It was our task to prove our ideas really worked, and in this context "working" meant achieving the intentions of the plan with a way of building that was as dense, as rapid, and no more expensive than the deeply entrenched standard way of doing business.

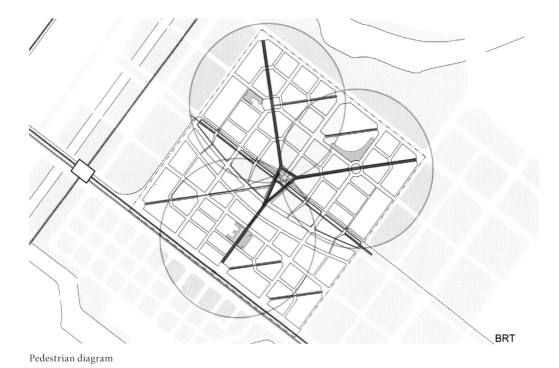

Pedestrian diagram

The Demonstration Neighborhood

This is the point at which many architects are used to becoming subversive double agents for the things they believe in, sneaking surreptitiously behind enemy lines, blending with the techno-bureaucrats, matching them metric for metric, and trying to beat them at their own game, all the while playing a different and far more interesting game. Hou Bin, a wily veteran at this sort of thing, of course knew exactly what we were up to.

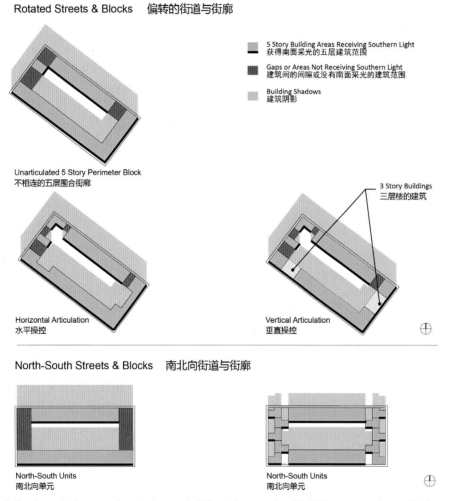

Left column: Red area receives inadequate daylight with conventional building types; perimeter blocks not possible. Right column: Reduces red area with building articulations; perimeter blocks achievable

We knew that we had to develop a system for producing our complex blocks, and the system had to be as simple to understand and communicate, as simple to build and to replicate, as the standard rows of mindless flats. At some point in our youth we were trained to think as rational modernists, so we knew what to do. We began by imposing a three-dimensional grid on our typical blocks. The grid established standard widths for one-, two-, and three-bedroom units and permitted variations in the depth of units to accommodate apartments of different sizes and level of accommodation: market rate units deeper, low income units shallower, but all the same widths and therefore interchangeable.

In our meetings with our clients, we soon discovered that one of Huo Bin's planners was an absolute monomaniac about plumbing that ran straight, especially vertically. He went absolutely berserko if he discovered what he thought was the need for a bent plumbing run in the plans. He was the plumbing guy, and he didn't seem to care about anything else—one insistent voice in the large chorus of techno-bureaucrats.

Our nifty new system enabled us to stack one-, two-, and three-bedroom units in different combinations and always have the structural walls and plumbing running straight vertically. The system can step, to permit daylight to penetrate the blocks, and it permits units to be omitted at the lower two or three floors to create passageways large or small from the streets to midblock courtyards or gardens. All of this is the kind of rational systematizing that infatuated Catherine Bauer at Ernst May's Romerstadt, but here it was directed at much richer and more complex patterns of urbanism.

A big part of our system is the plans of the apartments themselves. The work involved visiting many built projects in Tianjin and Binhai. After hours of looking at tiny, depressing, almost identical apartments, one's eyes tend to glaze over, but suddenly on one of these outings we came across an apartment no bigger than the others that had some brilliant, simple features that totally transformed it. This unit became our inspiration and our standard.

It had the ubiquitous south-facing living room, and the typical closed kitchen room to contain cooking smells. But a clever offset to the kitchen, an entry vestibule next to the kitchen, and a big glass sliding door to the kitchen, worked together to provide north light as well as south light in the main space, and cross-ventilation. South light only is raw glare, causing eye strain and turning the views into silhouettes without detail. This lovely apartment with soft, balanced light and fresh, natural ventilation became our template. After some study, we discovered that we could replicate the essentials of this plan in units of all sizes and that they could stack vertically within our grid in ways that satisfied even the plumbing guy.

Studio

1 bedroom apt.

2 bedroom apt.

3 bedroom apt.

Section

So after some months of study, we had nailed it. We had the bones of a system—highly standardized, easy to build, easy to communicate, and richly varied in the urban patterns one could make with it. We had our own Lego blocks to play with, but Lego blocks that contained simple patterns of structure, plumbing, daylighting, and pleasant, livable apartments of varied sizes. With 3-D computer modeling and a daylighting program, we could flesh out the armature of the master plan with compositions of urban blocks that placed tall buildings where we wanted them in relation to parks and transit hubs, and created the networks of courtyards, lanes, passages, and pedestrian life that we imagined. When the computer model was well along, we used the great resource of the physical model shop at Leon Huang's office, HHD, in Tianjin to build superb models at the scale of the demonstration neighborhood and at the scale of some typical blocks.

When this was done, Huo Bin convened a symposium of highly credentialed, extremely bright and articulate senior officials to review the work and (he hoped) endorse it enthusiastically as a welcome new pattern with profound implications for Chinese neighborhood planning. This they did in gracious and extravagant terms.

So far so good. Then events transpired that we that we had no way of understanding. For a while there was considerable discussion about what the next steps should be and whether we should shift our attentions to a different site that was out of the Port of Binhai jurisdiction, because some port officials did not want to get tangled up in the development business. Then suddenly there was a

1 bedroom apt.

4 bedroom apt.

2 bedroom apt., corner

2 bedroom apt.

Floor plans

terrible disaster on port land, very near our site—a huge explosion at a chemical storage facility that for a couple of days was headline news around the world. The political fallout from the disaster completely paralyzed all new initiatives in Binhai.

Ultimately, after months of silence, there was a small trickle of news about the fate of our Hexie. Huo Bin encouraged Leon Huang to submit the plan for a national planning award, which it received. At the same time, our good friend, Berkeley city planner Peter Calthorpe, working with the sponsorship of the California Energy Foundation, produced model legislation, not for specific neighborhood designs but for the larger infrastructure patterns of roads, transit, and development parcels that would break the deadly stranglehold of giant superblocks. Calthorpe, working from macroscale downward, and we, working from microscale upward, arrived at mutually supporting conclusions about the social and environmental disaster of Chinese planning laws and what to do about it.

Leon Huang took the Hexie show on the road to conferences and, wherever possible, to planners, developers, and public officials, promoting the Continuous City street grid, walkability, and small blocks as a new model for future Chinese cities, abandoning the gated community superblock model. The Hexie project was extensively used to illustrate the feasibility and benefits of the open city street grid system. The main points of this research were presented to the central government's Urban Task Force Committee in 2015. Our voices added to others appear to be having a profound effect. In February 2016, these ideas were embraced at the highest levels of Chinese officialdom, which

Residential street

Bicycle/pedestrian mixed-use street

Neighborhood center

announced a new policy forbidding building gated communities all over China, and establishing new national planning standards for small blocks, walkability, and transit-related design.

This does not mean that our Hexie plan is going to be implemented intact next week, but the tide is shifting in China. The issues of air quality in the Ruptured City of giant superblocks, and the hideous congestion they cause, weigh more heavily politically than the cultural loss of the life of the hutongs. But it is all connected. Like so many places in the world, the Ruptured City of Hope has lost its luster, while memory of the Continuous City—the little lanes where everyone knew everyone: the children, the old men at mah jong, the people who make things—has a haunting new presence. It will take time and many voices to shift the momentum of China's development juggernaut, but it seems inevitable that the Continuous City will return to China.

Passages and courtyards, urbanity rediscovered

PART II: TWO BATTLEGROUNDS

Paris and Rome.

Everybody visits Paris and Rome.

Everybody studies Paris and Rome.

Everybody studies almost everything about Paris and Rome,

except almost nobody studies the Continuous City and the Ruptured City

in Paris and Rome.

With a little bit of excavation, the student of cities can find stories of the epic battles between the Continuous City and the Ruptured City amid urbanism's greatest treasures

in Paris and Rome.

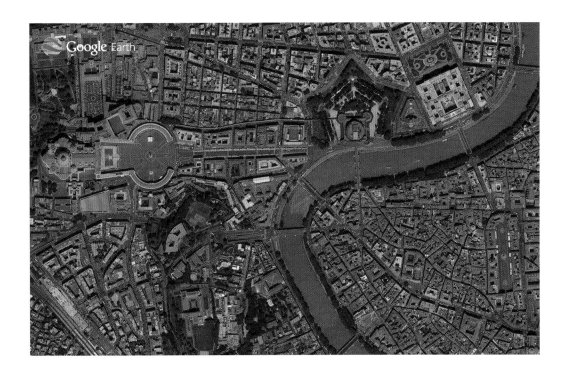

Cite'de l'Architecture et du Patrimoine, permanent exhibit

CHAPTER 11
PARIS: Two Pasts, Two Presents

We must pay a visit to Paris.

Two Ideas

In Paris, warfare between the City of Love (the Continuous City) and the City of Hope (the Ruptured City) has been so violent that it takes over CNN News every couple of years and the stories are broadcast around the world. Nowhere are the felicities of the Continuous City more adored by residents and millions of visitors, and nowhere has the City of Hope—the Ruptured City—turned out quite so badly, or with such destructive force.

Paris is the only city where the antagonists in the historiographical war each have erected a large museum devoted to the city's physical history, and they present skillfully, and with big budgets, completely different historical narratives. The war of ideas that has played out so dramatically in the city itself is also a propaganda war embodied in these two museums.

First is the Cité de l'Architecture et du Patrimoine, in the Pallais Chaillot, which opened in its current form to great fanfare in 2008 with President Nicholas Sarkozy himself basking in its luster. The museum was originally founded as the Musée National des Monuments Français by Eugène Viollet-le-Duc, nineteenth-century architecture's master poet of emerging technology. The ghost of Viollet-le-Duc floats all through the building, as if he were the permanent curator, with his spiritual precursors and descendants constituting the collection and many exhibits.

The entry level contains a beautiful permanent exhibit called *Patrimoine*, a highly edited history of French architecture from about AD 1100 to about 1550, when the intricacies of High Gothic building slowly emerged from French Romanesque. The *Patrimoine* exhibit ends with an exquisite series of small analytical models that explain the tectonics of Gothic structure—models so fascinating that they are bound to kindle the ambition to be architects or engineers in legions of bright ten-year-olds for generations to come.

At the end of the *Patrimoine* exhibition, you take a little elevator to the other half of the permanent exhibition, *Architecture Moderne* et *Contemporaire*. The terms moderne and contemporaire are a provocative distinction that the exhibit itself makes no reference to, apparently considering these words to be eternal synonyms. The elevator from *Patrimoine* delivers you to, of all things, an analytical model of that sacred cow in modernism's patrimony, Joseph Paxton's 1851 Crystal Palace in London. The technique of the model, its fascination with prefabrication, iron, and structural clarity, vividly makes the point that there is a relationship between the models of High Gothic tectonics one has just left behind, and the emergence of a technology-based modern architecture. The sacred-cow status was conferred upon the Crystal Palace by the main historian/ theorists of modern architecture, Sigfried Giedion, Nicholas Pevsner, and Reyner Banham, all of whom treated it as the seminal masterpiece and birth mother of modernism.

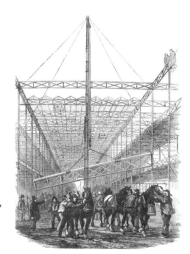

But wait a minute—what happened to the years between 1550 and 1851—the Paris of Henry IV to the Paris of Napoleon III? Weren't those the years in which the Paris that most people consider the glory of the world was built, the Paris everybody visits and writes songs about, where Gene Kelley and Leslie Caron made magic? Place des Vosges, Jardins du Palais Royale, the residential fabric of the 16th and the 7th Arrondissements, and all the rest.

Sacred Birth: the Crystal Palace

The exhibition continues from the Crystal Palace with analytical models of modern buildings in the same tectonic vein and concludes with a full-scale, two-story replica of an apartment from Le Corbusier's *Unité d'habitation* in Marsielles.

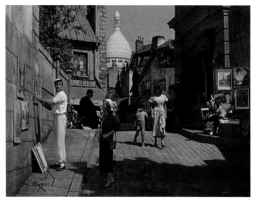

Icon: *An American in* (continuous) *Paris*; Gene Kelly and Leslie Caron

Along the way one encounters a clever little video animation that shows how each successive new technological era was accompanied by its own building typologies and city form—a glorification of revolutionary technical inventions with a focus on buildings, from masonry structures to iron structures, from low buildings with stairs to high buildings with elevators. One of the landmark inventions in the series is the automobile, and the video depicts how the sprawl of the Paris Peripherique and beyond is its logical outcome. The Cité story is a lurching, spasmodic history of technological change, with no apologies for what technology hath wrought, not even any mention of anything that might have gone wrong in the long march of technological determinism.

Another museum in Paris tells a very different story, the Pavilion de l'Arsenal. The Arsenal story is a continuous history of city building in relation to the city—a gradual accretion of complex adaptations and occasional upheavals, each in relation to predecessors, with a focus equally on buildings and the city itself. It begins with archaeological Paris—pre-Roman, then Roman, and it extends to all the latest things in and around Paris. It has a balanced appreciation for the positive contributions of modern architecture and recent urbanism, but with appropriate critical distance from excesses and failures. But mostly the exhibition focuses on the glories of Paris—Henry IV to Napoleon III, 1550 to 1850—the missing years in the Cité. It chronicles how project by project, building by building, regime by regime, the glories of Paris were constructed.

The conflict between these two stories is not an innocent sport played out on the benign turf of architectural historians. It is woven deeply into the actual fabric of the city, and it has erupted in violence, bloodshed, and paralytic social unrest.

The difference between these two traditions is not primarily about architectural style or the relationship of architectural style to "the spirit of the times." That is an altogether different debate, and it is important not to confuse the two. Where the two traditions stand in intractable opposition is their conception of what constitutes a legitimate generating force for architectural form. In the Cité tradition, architecture has a life force that comes from within—how it is made, its structural behavior, how it receives daylight. It is a highly appealing notion, especially to architects and those who aspire to be architects—buildings as little neo-Platonic microcosms of rational perfection or perfectibility. Thinghood.

In the other tradition, as represented at the Arsenal, buildings are never conceived except as part of something else, something bigger, like a city block or a street or a district.

The respective emblems of these two traditions are the slab block, which divorces the form of buildings from the form of streets, and the perimeter block, which marries them in intimate coexistence—Ruptured City and Continuous City.

Icon: slab block Paris

Ideas Realized

At various times, the French budget for social housing has been reputed to be larger than its budget for national defense, and whether that is exactly true or not, social housing has been a big deal in Paris and a major national political commitment since before WWI. Both points of view have had their chance at building social housing on a large scale, each resulting in many thousands of units in and around the city. The better-known story is that of Cité, a rational method applied to the problem, with an ancestry that extends from Le Corbusier and Ernst May back to Viollet-le-Duc. It is the story of the Grand Ensemble, the vast social housing program of the 1960s and 1970s that constructed scores of gigantic projects.

What most people know about French social housing is what happened in 2005, when three public housing projects far out in the northern suburbs of Paris erupted in violence that rapidly spread and brought the whole country to a standstill for many days. The images were broadcast

Clichy sous Bois, 2005

around the world, and many remember them. They are familiar folklore in France. They were foreshadowed ten years earlier with the 1995 Mathieu Kossovitz film, *La Haine* (*The Hate*), in which Clichy-sous-Bois, the very project where violence began in 2005, erupts in prescient cinematic riot.

The Grand Ensemble projects, including Clichy-sous-Bois, were built with great optimism, providing sunlight, air, and cleanliness to the slum-bound industrial working class of Paris and other cities. Three things were at work in shaping these projects.

Sun worship

Logique du Grue

City as art: Mondrian and Grand Ensemble

First was the provision of sunlight and air that the overcrowded old fabric of the city did not provide.

Second was something called *logique de grue*, the logic of the crane, technological determinism straight out of Viollet-le-Duc.

Third, there clearly was an aesthetic sensibility at work, because the Grand Ensemble site plans so resemble modern art of the 1920s and 1930s. These three considerations provided the rationale for setting the Grand Ensemble against the city, eradicating part of the old city or building far out in greenfields in clear distinction and opposition to the forms of Paris.

So what happened? In the 1960s and early '70s, many tens of thousands of working-class families moved into the Grand Ensemble, and as soon as they could afford to, they moved out. French working-class people in massive numbers hated the housing that the government had spent vast resources to provide for them. And what did they want?

Either they wanted to move back into the heart of Paris, where public housing had years-long waiting lists, or in large numbers they wanted traditional, small, low-density suburban houses.

As the Grand Ensemble projects were abandoned in the 1960s and '70s by those for whom they were built, they became virtual detention centers for France's ever-growing populations of immigrants and minorities: the flood of Algerian, African, Moroccan, and Middle Eastern newcomers.

There is widespread consensus that it was the isolation of the Grand Ensembles, and their architecture, that drove a wedge into the divisions of French society. In 2005, when the French public housing riots that began at Clichy-sous-Bois dominated the news, it was the only time I can think of that architecture was indicted for murder and inciting violence in the popular mind. The press even coined a word for the alienation and fury that young people in the projects felt. They called it *Sarcelliteé* after Sarcelles, one of the largest, grimmest, and most isolated projects. The hopeless alienation of immigrant populations in the Grand Ensemble continues to be associated in the French press with terror, seething hatred, and violence.

The American version of the story is Pruitt Iago in St. Louis, and the simplistic narrative about both it and the Grand Ensemble is that modernism failed; the social welfare state failed; therefore blow it all up. In France, as here, that simplistic narrative has some truth in it, but the actual story is more complex and nuanced.

It turns out that the Cité story not only ignores the four most important centuries of Parisian urban history, it ignores much of the present and the recent past, including a long, rich history of social housing that like the urbanism on display at the Arsenal is all built in relation to the city. This story is hardly known at all.

Foyer-Logement, Foundation Rothschild, 1913

Consider the following sequence of social housing projects built over a period of fifty years nestled into the typically Parisian 18th Arrondissement. The Foyer-Logement of the Foundation Rothschild is a beautiful courtyard apartment complex built in 1913 to the highest standard of Parisian elegance as low-income housing, today impeccably restored and maintained in its original use. Anyone familiar with the condition of what remains of American public housing one-third as old must marvel at the wisdom of the Foundation Rothschild's investment in excellence more than a century ago.

Championnet, 1965

Directly across the street from the Rothschild complex is another beautiful low-income project known as Championnet, built in 1965. It is astonishing that at the very time the Ruptured City Grand Ensemble projects were in full swing, there were Parisian architects with the highest level of Continuous City skills, and there were bureaucrats at the agency known as HLM or Habitation à Loyer

Moderé (Habitat at Moderate Rent) willing to give them major commissions. Championnet does everything right. It holds the curving street wall at the same height as the Rothschild building, with a crisply detailed, modern limestone façade that blends perfectly into the historic fabric. Behind the street building is an impeccably maintained courtyard, intensely used by children, mothers, and resident gardeners. In the middle block, set back and concealed from surrounding streets by the lower building, is a super-dense high-rise slab housing hundreds of residents and giving offense to no one. Every resident one speaks to at Championnet seems to exude pride of place and pleasure at living there, and they are the same multihued mix of immigrants that constitute the sullen denizens one sees trapped out in the Grand Ensemble. No mystery; who wouldn't like living in a beautiful building in a great neighborhood in the heart of Paris? There is a years-long waiting list.

These projects are not an isolated anomaly. Scattered through the 18th Arrondissement are big, dense, beautifully made apartment blocks, tens of thousands of units—mostly brick and limestone with intricate networks of courtyards and alleys built under the HBM (Habitacion Bon Marché) program in

Habitacion Bon Marché, circa 1928, 18th Arrondissement

the 1920s and '30s. The HBM are so essentially Parisian that one thinks of them as simply the fabric of the city, and not as low-income "projects" with all the nasty connotations of that word. Through the heyday of modernist Ruptured City propaganda, these superb Continuous City social housing projects were conceived and executed on a vast scale, a concurrent alternative history going on with great vigor.

Reformation and Reconciliation

The failure of Grand Ensemble thinking was obvious even before its construction ended. I don't know when the word *desenclavement* (opening up) was coined, but the French use it in relation to fixing the Grand Ensemble. Desenclavement means something like "dis-discontinuous-ing." The later phases of Sarcelles in the 1970s, and slightly later, Grand Ensemble projects such as Olympiad in the southern part of the city, already were making concessions to integration with the city and the problems of *Sarcelliteé*. Before the Grand Ensemble initiative ended, attempts to create pedestrian life with retail and community facilities became part of the program.

Desenclavement projects vary widely in approach, ambition, and quality. Some are superficial tartings up of terrible buildings; some, like Montfermeil, are major reconstructions that acknowledge the original sins.

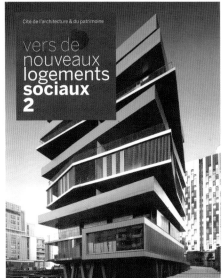

Montfermeil reconstructed: utopia vanquished (left)
But they don't give up: catalog from Cité de l'Architecture et du Patrimoine (right)

Montfermeil, one of the nightmare places that did everything wrong, is now transformed with great intelligence into a beautiful place. Long, long slab blocks are sliced up to become parts of perimeter blocks, shapeless space becomes defined space, disconnection becomes connection, something apart from the town becomes part of town.

One might say Montfermeil represents the surrender of utopian modernism to contextual urbanism. One could look at it and say simply that in the clash of ideas about regenerating the city versus replacing it, regenerating it has won and replacing it has lost. Hooray, hooray, the good guys won.

But not so fast. Look at the cover of the catalog from the recent show at the Cité. *Towards a New Social Housing*, it is called, celebrating "experimentation in an area which has been seen as an architectural laboratory since the beginning of the modern era."[1] Who, one wants to ask, are the mice in this architectural laboratory? Perhaps they are the next generations of sullen young men suffering from the next generation of *Sarcellité* or whatever it will be called the next time architectural hubris, utopianism, or the single-minded *logique-de-*something estranges people from the city they live in.

This Paris story is so compelling because it shows more clearly than anywhere the power of architectural ideas for good and for harm.

Paris offers us a record that is absolutely clear about the destructive power of ideas that have dominated and still dominate the main institutions of architectural culture—MoMA, Harvard, and *Architectural Record*, no less than the Cité de l'Architecture et du Patrimoine. In Paris those ideas were applied to many hundreds of thousands of housing units for the poor, with catastrophic results. In the same city and almost at the same time, the opposite occurred in hundreds of thousands of housing units for the poor. It is where the City of Love and the City of Hope have each made their own story, and where each tell their own story. One has only to look.

CHAPTER 12
ROME: Prologues

The Translucency of Fingers

In a dark room, if you cover a flashlight or reading lamp with your hand, you will see that light is transmitted only through your fingers. Whatever kind of light source you use, the light that comes through fingers (through, not around) is a brilliant, lurid orange. The rest of your hand and your body are opaque except to X-rays and MRI machines.

The phrase "the translucency of fingers" is so seductive, and the phenomenon itself so striking, that one is inclined to think there must be a potent metaphor lurking. If you believe that one thing can stand for another (some don't), then the intense orange light that emerges from human fingers must stand for something. If they had had flashlights or halogen reading lamps, the spiritual fathers of the arts and crafts movement, John Ruskin and William Morris, might have seized this image: the human soul transmitted to inanimate objects by the light that passes through the fingers of the craftsman. They made no such connection, perhaps because candles or gas lamps of their time gave off too much unfocused ambient light to illuminate fingers in the right evocative way.

I have another thought about that intense orange light. It is like the super-concentrated essence of the color of Rome, a color so garish, vulgar, and overwhelming in its pure state that it needs to be diluted ten thousandfold by time and life to assume its beautiful luminosity. The colors of Italian cities are usually attributed to the colors of local clays used for rendering buildings—the yellowish cast of Lucca, the umbers of Umbria, and so on. But the color of Rome, the incandescence that reverberates throughout the city, especially in the early morning and late afternoon, cannot be simply the reflection of dead clay. That glow must come through millions and millions of fingers over thousands of years, building and building.

The Choice

The dream took place in a very specific setting, a small lecture hall at the Sapienza Campus of the University of Rome. It was a gathering of PhD candidates in Roman history, and on this occasion each of them would be confronted with a terrible, life-altering choice. There were stacks of packages wrapped in a parchment-like substance, each the size and weight of a good-sized piece of cheese, about a kilo or a little more. The parchment wrappers were opaque and gave only the slightest hint of the texture, smell, and color of the contents. I guessed that the packages really were some sort of cheese.

At this meeting, each young student had to select a package, and the cheese within contained his or her life work. They had to select the cheese without really tasting it, and once made, the choice was inexorable, like a dissertation topic, but more binding and serious. A faculty advisor explained that while the cheeses tasted different, they were all good, safe choices except for one that appeared through its parchment wrapper to be rougher in texture and more pungent than the others.

Those who chose any of the other cheeses could be sure of a ready source of data for their research, a sympathetic peer review committee of people who had made similar choices and would understand their material, and in the end a very good chance for publication and employment. They would have to understand, however, that none of these cheeses would provide them with a comprehensive spiritual understanding of Rome. With any of the choices but one, they could be assured of a more or less satisfactory academic career, but they must accept the prospect of a gnawing sense of spiritual emptiness.

The cheese that appeared rough and smelly was altogether different. If any dared to choose it, they faced a lifetime of risk, the potential for ridicule, deadends in the paths of inquiry, profound intellectual loneliness. Their readings would be weird and eclectic, and their writing had no guarantee of an audience or even publication. Employment was unlikely because no institution had places for this type of cheese, and there was the matter of odor. The only thing the smelly cheese offered was a complete understanding of Rome—its millennia of secrets, the binding spirit that one senses in the streets but cannot name, the endless contradictions that never make sense, what the Roman light does to consciousness. The historical journey in the smelly cheese is a journey of the soul.

A whisper went around the room. Who had ever chosen the smelly cheese? What had happened to them? No one really knew, but there were rumors, speculations: Federico Fellini? Gustavo Giovannoni? Aldo Rossi? Anna Magnani? Spiro Kostov? Marcello Mastroianni? Christian Norberg-Shulz?

Before the candidates made their choices, I awoke into the hard rational light of morning. I'll never know what happened.

Romanità

It is a phenomenon that I have noticed subliminally for years without ever articulating it to myself; then on a recent Roman walk, it really struck me. The walk took me down the long block of Vicolo San Onofrio, near the Vatican. The steep street is narrow, there is no traffic, and one is so close to the buildings that all you see are their textures, colors, and material—the distinctive, pervasive Roman palette: travertine trim made richer by blackish grime, layers of peeling brownish or reddish or orangish stucco rendering, the warm gray and roughness of the revealed rubble masonry beneath, bits of black and dark brown bronze or wrought iron, well-varnished wood.

As I was contemplating this collage, two men came walking up the steep street. They were dressed in lots of layers, as ordinary Roman *ragazzi* dress on a winter day—parka, jacket, sweater, shirt, and skillfully tied scarves. They were layered like the building next to us with its century or more of patina, and in exactly the same rich, muted palette: browns and dark red, black and warm gray, dun green like the winter trees above the other side of the street.

Romanità, the Continuous City, is a remarkably deep phenomenon. It penetrated the souls of these two guys as they dressed in the morning, just as it has penetrated the souls of the best architects working in the city for centuries.

CHAPTER 13

ROME: The Continuous City Achieved and Abandoned

Rome gets under your skin and haunts your dreams. It is so complex, so beautiful, so layered with contradictions, that unraveling its intertwined stories becomes a compulsion. No other city has so many institutions devoted to the study of itself; it is the solipsistic city.

There is also no modern city with a longer or richer culture of building than Rome. There is no city where the act of building has repeatedly assumed such colossal political importance or achieved such heights of refinement—from antiquity to the present. There is no other place where the student of human settlements can learn so much; it is the urban textbook par excellence.

Rome is one of the most adored and certainly the most studied place in the world—from eighteenth-century travelers to twenty-first-century PhD candidates, no other city has been the focus of such scrutiny and love. There are more drawings, more maps, more photographs of Rome than any place on Earth, and generation after generation of students arrive from all over to churn them out. But 99.9 percent of that attention has been lavished on the 5 percent of the city built prior to the twentieth century. Very few students of cities have paid much attention to the last hundred years of this large, exceptionally agreeable living metropolis—how it is organized, how it was built, and why, despite the usual list of urban problems, much of it is an eminently good place to live.

There are reasons for this lopsided focus. First, historic Rome is a reliquary like no other, with the very foundations of Western civilization spread over and under its seven hills. These treasures are what draw the legions of visitors and scholars. Second, there is a political taboo. For more than sixty years, and until very recently, it has been inadmissible to say that anything positive in the realm of policy was accomplished during the Fascist years. To claim that many of Mussolini's acts of city building produced far more livable places than what came along later has been a double apostasy—first against the fallen of Monte Cassino and Anzio, and second against the form of Ruptured City promoted by hegemonic modernism.

Generations of Anglo-American architects have learned different lessons in Rome. Arthur Brown came to Rome and saw Carlo Rinaldi. The results were the great neoclassical buildings of San Francisco. Louis Kahn came to Rome and saw the bricks of Carracalla. The results were Kahn's timeless modern masterpieces. Robert Venturi came to Rome and saw the mannerists, Baldassare Peruzzi, and Giulio Romano. His results were the seminal text *Complexity and Contradiction in Architecture*, and a long career of buildings of inimitable wit. Colin Rowe came to Rome and saw Via Giulia and Piazza dei Popolo. From this came the hugely important Cornell Urban Design Studio and the great textbook *Collage City*. Of course, all of them came to Rome and saw all of it, but the special parts of Rome that struck them in the heart shaped their lives and legacies. We can come to Rome and see the Continuous City and the Ruptured City and also be struck in the heart, because nowhere else did each assume such potency as political symbols. As in Paris, the contrast between them is vivid instruction to lovers of cities.

The story of Rome in the twentieth century is essential to the theme of Love versus Hope. The great urban drama of gigantic personalities acting on the stage of Rome's politically tumultuous twentieth century, with historic Rome as the backdrop, demands a fully developed volume of its own. That companion volume is titled *The Splendid Ordinary: Roman Neighborhoods, 1909–1982*, which I am coauthoring with historian Jean-Francois Lejeune and Professor Lucio Barbera, former dean of the School of Architecture, University of Rome at La Sapienza. However, the Love versus Hope story would have a giant hole in it without a brief excursion to Rome, viewed through the lens of the Continuous City / Ruptured City. Consider this chapter an introduction to *The Splendid Ordinary*.

To simplify and understand the broad outlines of a complicated history, it is possible to divide the last century of Roman urbanism into two sharply different eras—1909 to 1960, and 1960 to the present. In the early 1960s, the laws and customs that had produced five decades of egalitarian, sometimes magnificent Continuous City in Rome gradually unraveled to produce its opposite. The very finest Roman architects were part of the unraveling, not as passive bystanders but as passionate partisans. They devoted their formidable skills, energies, and amazing survival instincts to coating this cultural unraveling with the gloss of high achievement. Leading Roman architects of the postwar years—Adalberto Libera, Luigi Moretti, Mario Fiorentino, and, above all, Ludovico Quaroni—were aristocrats of the architectural culture of Rome, princelings in the feudal hierarchies that governed the building of the city for generations. By 1960, they were all consumed according to the diktat of those times with their own *thinghood*—with newness, not continuity. In 1962, a new General Plan for Rome supported their new preoccupations by substituting the vagaries of American sprawl-style land-use planning for the typological (or form-based) zoning that had given structure to Roman neighborhoods for many decades. Rome's two very different modern half centuries are an irresistible match to our larger theme—the Continuous City and its antitype, the Ruptured City. This conflict is universal, but the splendor of history's record in Rome gives it special poignancy and clarity.

Virtually all the residential fabric built in Rome between 1909 and 1960 fits the description of Continuous City, and most of the large-scale housing built since then is discontinuous. This cultural and urbanistic upheaval is a largely untold story that must be assembled from fragments. Perhaps its most fascinating chapter is the very moment of transition, when the Continuous City and the Ruptured City, the City of Love and the City of Hope, lived together for a while in a brief, tenuous equilibrium. Understanding that short and almost completely ignored period of truce may be the key to applying Rome's mysterious secrets to cities everywhere.

Like other eras of Roman history, the city's chapters of Love versus Hope are the stories of people. There is no separating architectural and political history from biography. To understand what happened, we must (like Edward Gibbon, *The History of the Decline and Fall of the Roman Empire*) look at individuals who shaped events. Our companion volume, *The Splendid Ordinary*, will offer a much more extensive chronicle of events and people, but the bare bones of the story demand familiarity with four extraordinary characters.

Here's our group: Camillo Sitte, Gustavo Giovannoni, Marcello Piacentini, Margherita Sarfatti.

Camillo Sitte

A place to start the story of the Continuous City phase of modern Rome is with the publication of *City Building According to Artistic Principles* (*Städtebau Nach Kustlerishe Grundreise*), by Austrian theorist Camillo Sitte in 1889. It is perhaps the foundational document of the Continuous City. Sitte's influence was widespread in England, the US, Germany, Belgium, the Netherlands, Spain, and Scandinavia, and it appeared and reappeared in Rome in different guises. Sitte's subject is the European city, especially the informal, spontaneous compositions of streets and squares that were the product of anonymous builders over centuries.

There is more than one way to read Sitte. You can dismiss him and think of him in the conventional way as generations of Ruptured City modernists have—as the essential kitsch-mongering cornball reactionary who wanted to impose medievalism on modern life.

Alternatively, you can read Sitte's city drawings and the accounts of his city walks (many were in the remnants of medieval Italy) as a thoroughly modern interest in perception, experience, and time. This reading places his *Städtebau* close to the revolution in modernist fiction that appeared twenty years later in James Joyce and Marcel Proust, and allies it with cubist painting's collapsing of time and multiplication of viewpoint. Sitte's urban walks, with their infinite stream of the particular, fit squarely in time and spirit between Dickens's walks through London and Joyce's walks through Dublin. The difference is that Sitte's descriptions are drawings, not prose.

Städtebau was published in the same year as Thomas Edison's first motion picture, and Sitte had a way of viewing the city as pictures—constantly changing, complex, ever-composed pictures as one moves through time and space.

For Sitte, the continuity of the city is what gives meaning and coherence to movement through it. Buildings are meaningful to the degree that they sustain and punctuate the constantly unfolding experience of the city as sequentially composed pictures. He utterly deplored what he assumed would be the short-lived and ridiculous fad for freestanding architecture. Sitte's idea of continuity is both spatial and temporal; it embraces the continuous fabric of the European city and the deep heritage of vernacular architecture—both anathema to the Ruptured City hegemony of the next generations.

Gustavo Giovannoni

Sitte's link to modern Rome was Gustavo Giovannoni, a gigantic figure in the expansion of the city. Giovannoni was a planner, preservationist, architect, scholar, educator, charismatic leader, political operative, and power broker, and a Roman to the core. He was a founder and director of the school of architecture at Rome, La Sapienza, in 1920 and served as dean from 1927 to 1935. He was mentor to many who became the great names in Italian architecture before and after WWII.

The years after Rome became the new capital of a new nation were a tempest of cultural confusion and pressing need. What did it mean to be a functioning modern city? A European city? A grand capital with a glorious past? In this swirl, the calming, authoritative presence of Gustavo Giovannoni emerged. He was trained as an engineer but was a broadly cultured person who expanded his interests to architecture and urbanism. He also authored scores of publications that analyzed historic parts of Rome and other cities with beautifully drawn figure/ground plans and sequential perspective views, which were reminiscent of the vision and representation methods of Sitte's *Städtebau*. Giovannoni did many things in a long, complex career, but one of his contributions was bringing Sitte to Rome.

Giovannoni was born in 1873, thirty years after three men whose powerful sensibilities one can find in his work and scholarship. First was Sitte. The second was the superb watercolorist and recorder of urban scenes Ettore Roesler Franz, who was active and well known in the small Roman community of Giovannoni's youth. In 1881 Franz first exhibited his loving record of pre-1870 Rome, just as much of it was vanishing. In scores of luminous paintings, over many years, he showed a large pastoral village woven through the ruins of antiquity. In great detail, he recorded the daily life and the totally informal, well-worn charm of the vernacular architecture of the big village. Though he can't have known of Sitte, his conception of the city as an endlessly unfolding sequence of beautifully composed pictures has much in common with *Städtebau*. His fascination with the homely detail of the lives and dwellings of common people reappeared a half century later as neorealism in Italian literature, film, and architecture. It should be noted that Roessler Franz was enchanted with decrepitude, partially because it was in the act of disappearing, while Sitte and Giovannoni saw a humane and progressive role for the picturesque in making the modern city.

The third sensibility one can find in the work of Giovannoni is that of the great German urbanist Josef Stübben. In 1909, Giovannoni invited Stubben to Rome to work with him on the plan for the Piazza Mazzini district, one of Rome's major twentieth-century neighborhoods. With Stübben, he shared two apparently contradictory enthusiasms—first for Sitte and second for Georges-Eugené Hausmann and his grandiose transformations of Paris. The monumental and the picturesque somehow managed to cohabit the complex minds of both Giovannoni and Stübben. This unending tension between modernity (Hausmann) and memory (Sitte) was to play itself out for the next fifty years in Rome, for the most part to the eternal benefit of the eternal city.

Marcello Piacentini

The other dominant figure in the building of modern Rome was Giovannoni's friend and colleague Marcello Piacentini— an architect of protean talent: a modernist, a classicist, able to think boldly at the scale of the city and able to craft individual buildings with exquisite skill. Both Giovannoni and Piacentini were well-established figures when Benito Mussolini came to power in 1922. Perhaps the best administrative decision Mussolini made in his tumultuous twenty-two-year regime was to invest both of them with enormous power and responsibility for the expansion of Rome. It is important to note that Piacentini had secured his identity as an architect long before the Fascist ascendency. It grew from many sources, including his love and knowledge of Nordic classicism and its resonance with Roman history. For him, Nordic classicism translated into Italian materials and adapted to the Italian climate, representing a compelling "third path" between nineteenth-century revivalism and the modernist experiments in Germany, France, and the Netherlands—a way for Italy to be both modern and true to its history. Mussolini was an appreciative patron, to be sure, but it is not a misnomer to call Italian architecture from the 1920s until 1943 the era of Piacentini.

Undoubtedly, Margherita Sarfatti, Mussolini's Jewish mistress and hugely influential cultural advisor, played a role in his ascendency. It was Sarfatti who saw in Piacentini's architecture the symbolization of the Fascist regime as a modern Roman Empire. The look and built legacy of Italian Fascism may owe more to her than to anyone. In the later years of the Fascist regime, Giovannoni dared to oppose Mussolini's grandiose demolitions in the city center, and he fell from favor, but the marks that Giovannoni and Piacentini made on modern Rome are huge and indelible.

After the war, Piacentini was assigned to a special tier of the underworld, a very deep one reserved for leading Fascists, but his influence did not end. Master plans for major neighborhoods such as Tuscolano and Parioli from the Piacentini-led Piano Regolatore of 1931 continued to be built until the tumultuous year 1960. By various combinations of chicanery, penitence, hypocrisy, and irrepressible talent, many of the architects who flourished under Piacentini's patronage—even Piacentini himself—continued to work after the war, both in practice and, for some, in the most prestigious academic appointments.

For centuries, the Romans of antiquity feared that the culture of Rome would be eradicated by barbarian hordes from the North. That ancient fear was somewhat like what many Americans of the 1950s felt toward Communists. In fact, the ancient Roman fears, like ours, never quite materialized. As Gibbon and many subsequent historians agree, Roman institutions and culture persevered well into the Christian era, and the changes from antiquity to medieval Rome were gradual.

Marcello Piacentini felt the same sort of apocalyptic fear of sudden cultural eradication as ancient Romans, directed at what he called "transalpine rationalism."[1] He could tolerate Italian modernists, of the Giuseppe Terragni, Adalberto Libera, Gruppo 7 sort, or the architecture of the new town of Sabaudia by the Gruppo degli Urbanisti Romani. But for him, the Walter Gropius, Ernst May, Le Corbusier, Eric Mendelsohn crowd across the Alps were true barbarians who posed an existential threat to urban civilization. The Mediterranean sun would incinerate 2,000 years of culture through the glass walls of northern modernism. Piacentini's fears were intertwined with his own fierce antisemitism that long predated Fascism's embrace of Nazi racial policies. He thought northern modernism to be a Jewish conspiracy like Bolshevism.

If (a big if) one can put Piacentini's craziness on race and religion aside, he was not altogether wrong, as things turned out. The transalpine rationalist barbarian hordes that terrified him fought (and won) on multiple fronts. They were the same people as the transatlantic rationalist barbarian hordes who built formidable redoubts at Harvard, at New York's Museum of Modern Art, and in Washington, DC. From there they launched devastating attacks on American cities as far away as San Francisco, causing permanent damage. The stories of Rome and San Francisco come together at many points.

Margherita Sarfatti

Franklin Delano Roosevelt had the great Harry Hopkins by his side.

Benito Mussolini had Margherita Sarfatti.

Hopkins was practically Roosevelt's roommate in the White House, living in the presidential quarters across the hall from FDR's bedroom. He was central to almost all that FDR achieved, in peace and war. Hopkins was a reclusive, often sickly man, and, though his role is no secret, he is not celebrated for the full scope of his brilliance, heroism, and influence.

Margherita Sarfatti's story is of similar magnitude, but until the publication of *Il Duce's Other Woman*[2] by American scholars Phillip Cannistraro and Brian Sullivan, it was almost completely unknown. For reasons that will become clear, Mussolini, before the end of his life, made a concerted effort to erase every trace of her from the historical record.

Sarfatti was a wealthy, high-born Venetian Jew educated by distinguished private tutors, surrounded from early youth by Europe's intellectual and artistic elite. By her early twenties she had established herself as a highly respected voice in art criticism and a passionate champion of modernism. For sixteen years, this elegant, refined person was the mistress of the rough-hewn Mussolini. They met in Socialist circles in Milan in the tumultuous time after WWI, and Sarfatti saw something—some power and potential—in this handsome, scarcely educated would-be political journalist.

The evolution from Socialist orthodoxy to the ideology of Fascism was a joint project of Sarfatti and Mussolini. Sarfatti and her lawyer husband were instrumental in the transformation of her lover from political observer to political actor. Most importantly for our story, it appears that Sarfatti more than anyone is responsible for the central conceit of Fascism as regards the city, the past, and the future. We can attribute to Sarfatti the idea—the complex and paradoxical idea—of the Fascist state as the reincarnation of the Roman Empire in modern technological times. This simultaneous embrace of past, present, and future set the stage for the building of modern Rome and for the Continuous City as a political artifact of the highest order. Hitler had to find the glories of a mythological Germanic past in the make-believe of Wagner's operas, but Mussolini had the incomparable glories of a real antiquity all around.

By 1930, in much of Northern Europe, the traditional European city was seen as the enemy of modernism, as impediment to a rational, scientific, egalitarian society. In contrast, this hostility to the historical city was never a component of the great push for modernization that occurred in Italy in Fascist times. Reconciliation of modernity and antiquity was the very heart of the Fascist dream that Sarfatti did much to craft.

One cannot fail to be impressed by the shrewdness with which Marcello Piacentini and Margherita Safatti shaped their respective personas to align their mutual ambitions. Sarfatti saw in Piacentini's talents Roman grandeur in modern dress; Piacentini made sure that she did.

From the formation of the Fascist Party until Mussolini's catastrophic alliance with Nazi Germany in 1935, Sarfatti was mistress, mentor, cultural advisor, and power broker par excellence. Varied artistic movements of great sophistication flourished in Italy under Fascism, while city planning and architectural commissions were awarded to the finest architects. Mussolini can be credited with the very good sense to defer to her in these matters. Ultimately, Sarfatti and other Fascist intellectuals lost the battle to align Italy with the Allies—France, England, and the US—against Hitler. As a Jewess, she was forced to flee, first to Paris, where she visited her friends Jean Cocteau and Coco Chanel, then to South America, where she survived the war in style and comfort, returning to Italy in 1947.

Our four big personalities belong to a longer list of people who created a phenomenon no other city has quite equaled. From the time the scruffy little village nestled in the splendors of historic Rome was declared the capital of Italy in 1870, until it reached its population peak close to three million in 1980, the growth of Rome was planned and executed by its most learned and sophisticated architects, planners, and academics. There is perhaps no other city where there is such close correspondence between shifting ideals of the city, its theory, and its built, lived-in realty.

There is no other city where such refinement of skill and sensibility was directed at the Continuous City for such a long time at such a grand scale. Rome is the finest textbook of the Continuous City, but it currently has very few readers. Rome also had its unique and fascinating interregnum, where for a brief time, the modernist ideals that generated the Ruptured City worldwide, and those especially Roman Continuous City skills, lived in fragile harmony.

Our companion volume, *The Splendid Ordinary: Roman Neighborhoods, 1909–1982*, will attempt to fill a glaring void of English-language scholarship on twentieth-century Rome with a survey of the urban morphology, architecture, intellectual underpinnings, and human stories behind an extensive list of Roman districts built in those years. What follows are some brief highlights from that list to secure Rome's central place in the Love versus Hope drama.

PREWAR: THE CONTINUOUS CITY ACHIEVED IN MULTIPLE WAYS

Garbatella

In the early 1920s, after the deprivations of WWI, Italy was experiencing what China is going through now: massive migration of impoverished rural people to new industrial and administrative employment in burgeoning cities. Mussolini shrewdly saw a basis for broad populist support in proposing housing programs for these people, rather than continue to urge them to emigrate. The Italian populations of North and South America owe their provenance to pre-Fascist Republican Italy's desire to decant potential sources of political unrest. Mussolini thought otherwise.

Garbatella figure/ground

The most dramatic early encounter of Camillo Sitte's thinking with Rome and with these pressing issues of social housing is the Roman neighborhood Garbatella. In 1920, Giovannoni and Massimo Piancentini (relative of Marcello) planned the first phase with loosely formed blocks of housing centered on the first public space, Piazza Brini. This small beginning established the urban morphology and architectural spirit for the next decades of construction by many hands. Garbatella was originally intended as worker housing for a new river port directly across the Tiber that never materialized. The district became a principal relocation site for thousands of Roman slum dwellers displaced by Mussolini's huge demolitions in the city center.

Garbatella scene

At Garbatella, Sitte's urban space and deep respect for vernacular building traditions are put to work with high social and political purpose, creating a familiar, welcoming place for displaced Romans and rural immigrants, based on vernacular building traditions interpreted by sophisticated architects. Moving through Garbatella, it is Sitte's city as sequential pictures—scenes unfolding, handsome frame by handsome frame. But these pictures are packed with life—composed and contained places filled with children, family gatherings, growing vegetables, and places for commerce. It is a continuous spatial experience that every building, path, and garden contribute to. In its constant familiar references to the vernacular of the Lazio countryside, it is also continuous temporally and culturally. People belong to Garbatella, and it belongs to them.

The basic unit of Garbatella is the perimeter block of semicontinuous buildings, with the irregularity that Sitte favored generated by topography. Streets wind up the hills with ever-changing vistas, and blocks are pierced by walkways, staircases, terraces—safe, secure, beautiful, incredibly pleasant, and filled with life, to this day.

Giovannoni's favored architect for individual buildings was the astonishingly versatile and facile Innocente Sabatini. At Garbatella, he thoroughly mastered local rural vernacular and spiced it up with learned Roman references of all sorts—to antiquity, the Renaissance, Borromini, even to Eric Mendelsohn and futurism—rich and eclectic, but not pedantic. This extraordinary architectural skill wedded to an absence of stylistic dogma is one of the great principles of Rome's Continuous City neighborhoods.

Sabatini's works appear throughout Garbatella and also in other great neighborhoods of social housing built in the 1920s, notably Prati and Testaccio. His design for Edificio Maggior Mole, the largest building in the Giovannoni / Massimo Piacentini first phase of Garbatella, set the tone for other architects and for what came later. It is a festive, jokey, eclectic mishmash, at the borderline of crazy, and apparently Giovannini liked it that way, at least here.

Sabatini makes later witty, eclectic ironists like Robert Venturi or Charles Moore seem dour and sedate. He brings the Baths of Diocletian to Garbatella at the Bagni Pubblici, and Borromini to the neighborhood at the Cinema Teatro, and introduces Borromini to the futurists at the lavish Alberghi Surburbani (suburban hotels) built for dislocated Romans. Garbatella was under construction from 1920 until the late '30s.

Sabatini's Edificio Maggior Mole

At the top of the hilly site, Sitte picturesque meets Fascist *grandezza* in the truly great civic space of Piazza Damiano Sauli. In accord with Fascist ideology, the centerpiece is a wildly flamboyant middle school by Giovanni Brunetto, topped with a giant row of black bronze eagles, with the monumental church by Alberto Calza Bini deferentially to the side. In this recent picture, the piazza is the scene of a monumental middle-school water fight—all this teeming life in the midst of the cleverest, most discreet handling of automobiles in a public space anywhere. Such skill.

Water fight in Piazza Domiano Sauli

For ninety years, working-class Romans of modest means have fared pretty well in this version of the Continuous City.

Piazza Mazzini

If Garbatella is the product of the Sitte/Franz part of Giovannoni's complicated brain, the Piazza Mazzini district is where the Baron Haussmann side of him got its chance. In 1909, tiny Rome was under great pressure to accommodate tens of thousands of workers in the new national bureaucracies. Mazzini was an enormous tract of contiguous, publicly owned land at the edge of the city, fulfilling the essential conditions for Giovannoni to act out his Haussmannian dreams.

If we are visiting Rome to learn its special lessons for the Continuous City, it is quite permissible to ignore the radial heart of the Mazzini plan and the tortured story of how Giovannoni, then Piacentini, then Stuben, and then Giovannoni and Piacentini

Piazza Mazzini master plan, 1925

together arrived at their final version of a Haussmannian plan. This center of Mazzini is okay, but its rondpoint and tree-lined radial boulevards are executed much better all over Paris.

It is the truly Roman parts of Mazzini that are splendid. Where fake Paris ends and real Rome begins is a short block away from the piazza itself. Parts of the radial plan are small circumferential streets, more or less parallel to the piazza. These streets are magnificent—narrow (32 feet +-), constantly curving closed vistas, with six- or seven-story housing blocks, many of them built as social housing of a consistent and highly efficient typology. In their scale, detail, and color they evoke the grandeur of Renaissance and Baroque Rome's many splendid palazzi on narrow medieval streets in the historic center of the city familiar to tourists. The small, curving streets; the big buildings with rich, overscaled detail; and the Roman colors create a continuously unfolding panorama of pictures: this is the Sittesque side of Giovannoni, come to life at a grand urban scale. This theme of monumental Roman palazzi as workers' or middle-class housing on tiny, congested streets like medieval Rome occurs over and over in Giovannoni and Piacentini's twentieth-century Rome. It was a way of welcoming newcomers of modest means to Roman life, granting them full status as Romans; Roman grandeur as political art.

Prati and Testaccio

Just southwest of Mazzini, in the shadow of the Vatican, is the neighborhood of Prati, and farther south across the Tiber is Testaccio. Early versions of both were first conceived as plans for city expansion in 1873 (Testaccio) and 1883 (Prati). Most of these large neighborhoods were realized in a short period of intense building activity in the 1910s and especially the 1920s as parts of the Fascist regime's social housing program. The best parts of the Mazzini District hint at what Prati and Testaccio achieved on a massive scale—Roman splendor for middle-class bureaucrats (most of Prati) and the working class (Testaccio and the Trionfale section of Prati)—the Continuous City in all of its physical, temporal, and social dimensions. It is notable the degree to which these quite magnificent places are ignored in the literature of twentieth-century planning and in the extensive documentation of Fascist architecture. Even Spiro Kostof never mentions Prati and dismisses Testaccio with one cryptic and contemptuous sentence.

Postwar scholars and most other people are inclined to see Italian Fascism as caricature, often the self-caricature perpetrated by its most grandiose architecture and by the antics of Mussolini himself. I must admit that for much of my adult life my own images of Mussolini were shaped first by Jack Oakey's immortal comic portrayal opposite Charlie Chaplin's equally hilarious Hitler in Chaplin's *The Great Dictator*, and second by Winston Churchill's unforgettable cadences, which I memorized and spouted as a (no doubt obnoxious) eight-year-old and have carried in my head ever since:

Jack Oakey and Charlie Chaplin in
The Great Dictator

This whipped jackal Mussolini comes frisking to the side of the German tiger with yelps, not only of avarice, for that would be understandable, but of triumph. Surely this must be a world's record in the domain of the ridiculous and the contemptible.

When these caricatures swirl together with images of Black Shirt thugs, the horrors of the Holocaust, the Garden of the Fitzi Contini, and the supreme pomposity of monuments like Piacentini's main Sapienza Campus—then achievements like Prati and Testacchio just don't fit the picture we have of Italian Fascism. How could the regime we have learned to think of as unremittingly brutal, thoroughly ridiculous, or both have produced urban places that remain so beautiful and livable long after their political meaning has disappeared? Perhaps scholars ignore Mazzini, Prati, and Testacchio because they don't know what to make of them. Can one extol their virtues without painting oneself with the smelly brush of Neofascism? Perhaps one should just look at them, look closely, or better, live in these places for a while, which I have had the good fortune to do.

The word that describes the most Roman of Roman qualities is grandeur—the grandeur of antiquity, the grandeur of the popes, the amazing grandeur of the fabric of the historic center studded with the palazzi of the great dynastic families. With the construction of Prati and Testacchio, ordinary working people became the legatees of Rome's historic grandeur, and for whatever horrors Italian Fascism brought to Italy and the world, this much they got right.

There is a great irony here. The twenty-first-century revival of right-wing Neofascist politics in Italy and in much of Europe is based on anti-immigrant, nativist hysteria, but the capital of the longest enduring Fascist regime provided perhaps the best model of an urbanism of assimilation. Roman Fascists did for people they considered barbaric southern peasants something like what Romans of antiquity did for the Ostrogoths—they made Rome more Roman and welcomed the alien newcomers to this more Roman Rome.

Prati street scene

Morning in Prati

Before leaving the apartment, I adjust the windows. Everything was open to the Roman morning, with reflection off the tawny, sun-washed building across the street making beautiful light in the apartment. Before I get back it will be hot, so I close the shutters but leave the windows front and back open to the breeze.

I step into the tiny elevator with a ten-year-old with a backpack. Buon giorno. One floor down an elderly lady with a shopping cart crowds in. Buon giorno. Bouno giorno. Bouon giorno. Emilio, how is your foot? All better, no problem, thank you.

I go out of the building, turn left, and walk eleven steps to the café. The man making coffee shouts over to the cashier Un cappucino, e un corneto simplice. This is my first week here, and the coffee man already knows exactly what I like. The coffee is delicious; the corneto excellent—flaky, buttery, warm from the oven. Everyone seems to be a regular, and there are half a dozen conversations flying up and down the bar.

Next I go across the street to the store and ask for toothpaste. Down the steps and to the right. Colgate 2.5 euros, Pepsodent 2.5 euros, Pasta del Capitano 1.9 euros. I go for Pasta del Capitano. I go up the street and pass the trattoria with the outdoor tables being set for lunch. A man coming the other way asks the waiter if the clams are fresh today. Yes, beautiful clams just came in. Okay, the other man says, three at 1:30.

I stop on the way to the studio to buy a Herald Tribune *from the man in the magazine kiosk. I arrive to meet my students promptly at 9:30.*
Total distance covered since leaving the apartment: 350 meters
Total elapsed time: twenty-seven minutes
Conversations: four as participant, eight overheard
Such is life in the Continuous City.

POSTWAR: ANTI-FASCIST CONTINUOUS CITY

Tiburtino

The Tiburtino District began much later than Garbatella, Mazzini, Prati, or Testaccio. It is a public housing project built after WWII, between 1947 and 1954, contemporaneous with the great postwar period of Italian film known as neorealism. Since Tiburtino is commonly referred to as neorealist architecture and urbanism, it is appropriate to begin discussion of it with dramatis personae:

Ludovico Quaroni: Codirector of design for Tiburtino; the protege of Marcello Piacentini. Later head of the School of Architecture, La Sapienza

Mario Ridolfi: Codirector of design for Tiburtino, one of the most gifted Roman architects

Carlo Aymonino: Assistant to Quaroni and Ridolfi; nephew of Marcello Piacentini; later head of the School of Architecture, Venice

Camillo Sitte: Ghost presence.

Ettore Roesler Franz: Ghost presence

Note that contrary to the theory (not always the practice) of neorealist film, this is an all-star cast drawn from artistic and architectural aristocracy. Perhaps the most succinct way to convey the neorealist spirit is to quote from a savage skewering of the movement, written in 1948 by film director and critic Stefano Vanzina. This is from a passage titled "Inevitable Characters in a Neorealist Film."[3] In the Italy of 1948, this would have been immediately recognized as parody of the Fascist orders that disappeared from Italian life only four years earlier. The inevitable characters include:

The overweight father searching the whorehouses of the town for his daughter who vanished during an air raid . . . a priest bicycling toward the town of Comacchio. The village idiot (with a limp, lame, mute, and stuttering at the same time) who has fallen in love with the provocative wife of the postman . . . an accordion.

Neorealism was a celebration of antiheroes and the antiheroic; of the working class, the vernacular; of "real" life portrayed in real (as opposed to cinematic) time; of the struggles of ordinary folk in the shattered postwar society. It is the hundred-percent inverse of the heroic aspirations and pretentions of Fascism, and the movement provided safe ground for Italians eager to shed their Fascist raiment.

Ludovico Quaroni hardly seems a likely candidate for a starring role in a neorealist drama. Only three years before the beginning of Tiburtino, he was still at work on Piazza Imperiale at EUR, a determined effort by Quaroni and his partner Saverio Muratori to make something even more monumental, even more fascistic, than the heroic works of their mentor and patron—a can-you-top-this game of grandezza. The leap from Piazza Imperiale to Tiburtino is a never-before-attempted and never-equaled feat of ideological and stylistic trapeze artistry.

When you arrive at the original Quaroni/Ridolfi part of Tiburtino, you have stepped into a neorealist film. In 1957, Quaroni described it himself in words that verge on parody:
There were workers returning home with newspapers in hand, there were women making their final purchases for the next day in shops still lit up: in the darkness of the alleys burned the candles of the Via Crucis.

For me, as an architect who has struggled with the budgets of low-income housing for decades, I am immediately aware walking around Tiburtino of the pragmatism and extraordinary skill of these designers. It accomplishes everything they aspired to with the simplest of means and a few strategic manipulations of the most conventional of Roman housing types, the *casa in linea*. Quaroni and his collaborators knew how, not only to make a thoroughly convincing scenographic representation of an Italian village, but to make it a remarkably humane, practical, and pleasant living environment, and to do it on the cheap.

Tiburtino: perimeter blocks warped to topography

The *casa in linea* appears in all of the districts we visit in this chapter. It consists of rows of stacked flats paired around a common stair, sometimes with a third unit projecting from the stair. Because Roman fire regulations (like those typical throughout Europe) permit walk-up apartments to have access to only one stair, there is great flexibility in planning with the *casa in linea* as the basic building block.

Garbatella, Prati, and Testaccio all make use of clever manipulations of the *casa in linea* to create beautiful urban blocks, but those at Tiburtino are different and are especially tailored to the neorealist agenda. By introducing a diagonal wall to occasional stacks of units, the *casa in linea* can bend with a street grid that follows the topography, creating Sittesque sequences of views. Every now and then, usually at street corners, the stair emerges from the mass of the building and serves the second floor before disappearing inside. This costs a bit, but it evokes the vernacular buildings that Roesler Franz recorded in Trastevere and other medieval parts of the city, where multiple tenancies over time created the adaptive device of the outside stair. It is all part of the Tiburtino charm campaign. Also as in Roesler Franz's paintings, buildings sprout balconies, but just occasionally, and the top floors are articulated with loggias and pitched roofs. Some places a corner gets a little tower—seven stories of units paired around a stair, with the topography providing an entrance on the second floor so it can remain a walk-up (no budget for elevators).

A particularly clever (and much-photographed) group of apartments by Ridolfi's devoted protégé, Wolfgang Frankl, consists of two stories of townhouses stepping up a hill, over a tall story of ground-floor flats. The upper units are served by a grand stair that becomes a bridge. Between the shared stair/bridge and the upper units are little private gardens. Because the raised gardens are discontinuous, the lower flats get charming little entry courts, full of sunlight. These are complex and sophisticated manipulations that are really, really smart.

And all over Tiburtino there are shifts of color in a beautiful Roman palette.

If you spend time in Tiburtino and feel its rhythms—the bedding hanging from balconies, the clusters of men in endless conversation outside the corner bars, the kids roaming freely—it is impossible not to be seduced by the place. In 1958, avant-garde architects and Quaroni's own Sapienza students castigated Tiburtino as "a fake village, not a modern city."[4] Visiting it today, many years and many coats of stucco rendering later, one is struck by the realism of its neorealism. This skilled and conscious contrivance has the quality not of a stage set or a fake anything. It is a Roman lesson, not just in scenography, but in architecture and urbanism as loving study of the ordinary in the making of beloved places. Like Garbatella, this is love, not of Roman grandeur but of Roman folklore. There is more than one kind of Continuous City.

Palazzina figure/ground, Parioli

Half-breeds 2 and 3, Monteverde Nuovo and Parioli

In chapter 7 we visited Alfred Kastner's fascinating Carl Mackley Houses in Philadelphia, a handsome hybrid that mixed the genes of the City of Love and the City of Hope. On our tour of Rome we can find two more rare specimens of the ambiguous beauty of half-breeds.

For the sake of our argument, let us temporarily divide the immense complexity of Rome into some simple pieces. First there is the historic city—2,500 years of building and rebuilding, much of it made with the most refined and sophisticated intelligence ever directed at human habitat. For our purposes in this subchapter, let's just call all of that complexity one thing—Old Rome—and let's call its boundary the third-century Aurelian walls.

In our oversimplified categorizing, let's make the second category the Rome that was built between 1870, when the city became the capital of a newly unified Italy, and 1960, when Rome hosted the Olympic Games. During that time, Rome grew twentyfold as it transformed itself from a sleepy provincial village nestling in the glorious ruins to a large modern capital. There were momentous historic events during those ninety years—two world wars and the rise and fall of fascism. Through all that growth, turmoil, and change, however, Rome retained a steady commitment to the Continuous City, with echoes of Old Rome scattered throughout the new modern city, mostly outside the Aurelian walls.

In 1960, Rome made an abrupt and decisive rupture with its own past. The continuity with the ancient city from 1870 to 1960 and the ruptures of 1960 and beyond are subjects for the next sections, but for now let us focus on a sliver of time just prior to 1960, when tumultuous changes were just a rumbling portent, like Vesuvius in the days before the big day in AD 79.

In the great expansion of Rome, two planned neighborhoods, Parioli and Monteverde Nuovo, were built in the 1950s, just before the great watershed. Both succeed at reconciling the transalpine modernist obsession with daylight for everyone, with the walkable, interconnected fabric of the historic city. Changing circumstances created a short-lived moment of fragile equilibrium that produced these places of enduring quality.

The key to both of these somewhat different neighborhoods is a building type known as the palazzina, consisting of five or six stories of flats around a single stair and sometimes an elevator. In a typical palazzina, there are four apartments per floor, each apartment with abundant daylight all along two sides. The palazzina is always a freestanding building, though sometimes the ground floors are linked to form a continuous base along the street.* More often, the separations between buildings include the ground floor with small side yards, sometimes providing access to parking below, behind, or both.

The Parioli and Monteverde plans are very different. Parioli is built on a steep hill, and the streets follow the topography (unlike San Francisco), curving along the contours. Monteverde is also hilly, but the streets were laid out in the 1909 and 1931 general plans as a distorted grid with many irregularities and interruptions related to topography and edge conditions. The juxtaposition of grid and topographic interruptions is what Anne Vernez-Moudon observed and so admires in San Francisco.

Some things to note about these two neighborhoods:
— The principal planning regulation during the time that most of both districts were built was a designation of building type. The typological zoning laws mandated the freestanding house and the palazzina with its small side yards as the principal building type in most of both neighborhoods.

— Most of both districts were built after WWII, when almost all Roman architects were designing distinctly modern buildings. Monteverde has a sprinkling of prewar historicist architecture, but quite unlike Prati and Testacchio, which are deliberately ambiguous about when they were built, these districts are clearly modern, not historical Rome.

— Both neighborhoods were built by small-scale speculators on small subdivided parcels. Small lots and private speculation were anathema to the Far Left politics of the Roman architectural intelligentsia of the anti-Fascist postwar. For the radical students and faculty who hounded Saverio Muratori at Sapienza, the palazzina was beyond the pale. The academic crowd looked at these neighborhoods as low-brow developer schlock, right-wing and retrograde—so politically incorrect as to be unworthy of serious consideration.

*Note that American fire codes that require two ways of exiting every apartment in multistory buildings have made the palazzina or anything like it impossible in the US for many decades. It would be interesting to know, in the generations that palazzine have been common in Rome, whether anyone has ever been trapped in a fire because of the single stair.

The American Academy in Rome is right on the edge of Monteverde Nuovo, and the neighborhood's main street, Via Carini, is where academy fellows and visitors shop and do errands. The American Academy has had a steady stream of distinguished architectural and urban historians passing through it in the sixty-five years of Monteverde Nuovo's existence, but the academy's excellent library has not one word on the remarkable piece of urbanism that is literally next door.

Most of the buildings in Monteverde Nuovo and Parioli are decently designed and fairly well built—not masterpieces, but decent. Both neighborhoods do contain important works by architects of distinction, but these works reside quietly in the neighborhood fabric. They are not very different from what is around them—just better, with layers of subtle refinement their neighbors lack. The lovely streets of both neighborhoods can accept the presence of a masterpiece with no harm done either to the street or to the masterpiece.

One of Monteverde's Nuovo's fine, inconspicuous works consists of two city blocks of worker housing built under the INCIS subsidy program between 1914 and 1930, setting a standard for what came later. The architect was Fascist Party bigwig and dean of the School of Architecture at Naples, Alberto Calza Bini.

Calza Bini played the game of placing palazzina on the rectangular blocks like a chess master. The buildings are simple and straightforward, but they create sequences of beautiful spaces that cascade through the sloping sites in terraced communal gardens. The block perimeters are continuous street walls, broken but not too broken by the small side yards of the palazzina. At a strategic point there is a grand archway terminating a vista in a ceremonial entrance to the midblock gardens. These are modest buildings, constructed as low-cost housing, but everywhere one sees the hand of a sophisticated student of Old Rome. The apartments are now restored, desirable and expensive, partially because they reside in the light-filled palazzina building type.

It seems likely that the success of Calza Bini's INCIS project in Monteverde influenced Marcello Piacentini, who led the writing of the Rome General Plan of 1932 that mandated the palazzina as the principal building type for Parioli and the subsequent phases of Monteverde Nuovo. In Parioli, the famous masterpiece is Luigi Moretti's palazzina Il Girasole, a highly refined version of the typical palazzina, with a splendidly detailed central stair and carefully composed high modernist facades. It is normally surrounded by a steady stream of camera-toting international architecture students, most of whom never notice or understand that the Parioli district it is part of is a masterpiece of modern urbanism. They are, after all, architecture students, and thinghood is their thing.

Parioli aerial

The palazzina as a building type is an extraordinary invention that reconciles a fundamental conflict of the modern city: the urban street wall that defines the street as a public place where one might wish to walk, and abundant daylight for everyone who lives along that street. Parioli and Monteverde are extraordinarily pleasant places to live and to walk around. They are modern neighborhoods, connected into the city and completely free of the spooky, alienating quality of the isolated, high-modernist megaprojects that came later. These completely ignored hybrids with their simple street plans, small lots, continuous street walls, sunny buildings, and verdant streetscapes are among the best lessons and the best models that modern Rome provides.

The palazzina is a means (not the only means) of reconciling the utopian modernist obsession with equal daylight for all with the many charms and conveniences of traditional, walkable, sociable urban fabric. Parioli, Montverde Nuovo, and other parts of Rome that make use of the Palazzina accomplish this synthesis, but Monteverde Nuovo has other qualities that make it an urban design textbook.

It has geographic and historic advantages, and it may be serendipity or the genius of the master plan that the neighborhood uses them so well. Serendipity or not, the urban design lessons are clear. First, it is a good size for a neighborhood—about twenty minutes' walk north/south and five or ten minutes east/west. Second, except where it blends downhill to Monteverde Veccho and Trastevere, there are distinct edges: the magnificent and publicly accessible green parks, Villa Sciara and Villa Doria Pamphili, and beautiful sections of the Aurelian wall.

The southern end of Monteverde Nuovo is different from the rest and adds a fascinating layering of urban and social history to the neighborhood, beginning with three superbly designed, extremely dense courtyard blocks of INCIS public housing projects directed by Calza Bini and designed by Innocenzo Costantini and Pietro Sforz in 1931 and 1938. Many architectural and political themes join in seamless unity in these masterful buildings. They are decidedly "modern" and one sees the imprints of Italian futurism, German expressionism, and Eric Mendelsohn. They also have a highly propagandistic Fascist flavor—grandeur and optimism for working-class Romans. Spatially one sees in these modern buildings echoes of the Rome of the historic center:

courtyards linked by grand passages and arcades through and under buildings: modernity, Fascist grandiosity, and *romanità* combine to make a living environment much cherished by its working-class residents for generations.

Next door is another very different chapter: dense, nine-story INCIS public housing built in 1951, the product of the radically leftist postwar. Here the building type is the Continuous City's old nemeses, the Corbusian slab block, this time not set in vacuous open space but jammed into Roman fabric, holding street walls for blocks that are much too long and decidedly grim.

Then comes equally dense, privately developed middle-class infill, climbing up steep sites in curving Sittesque street scenes and enveloping the unfortunate slab blocks. One understands Camillo Sitte's fascination with the picturesque as a progressive element for the modern city. This southern section on and around Via di Donna Olimpia contributes a congenially working-class component to the otherwise middle-class Monteverde.

Unlike fancier Parioli, the neighborhood is studded throughout with small merchants, bars, bakeries, restaurants, churches, and schools. Street life is everywhere and everybody walks—children, dogs, old people, families. It is a great place to live one's life.

Palazzina streetscape, Monteverde Nuovo

Feeble Piazza, Villaggio Olimpico, 1960

THE RUPTURED CITY: LAW 167
Olympic Village

On a street corner next to the Circo Massimo, Imperial Rome's stupendous racetrack for chariots that Cecil B. DeMille was so fond of, is a quite good little restaurant. It serves a nice house white wine called "1960." The label on the bottle describes that year as a super-momentous date for three reasons: (1) the Rome Olympics, (2) the release of Federico Fellini's *La Dolce Vita*, and (3) the founding of the winery called "1960."

It is understandable that the owners of the winery consider their own birth date more worthy of inclusion in this triad than the ideological tumult in that year at the School of Architecture at Sapienza, but it is also significant that they list the Rome Olympics first. The Rome Olympics were a big deal—the chance for Italy to show the world that the echoes of Fascism and the struggles of *The Bicycle Thief* were long past. The earthy, hyperreality of postwar movie queen Anna Magnani gave way to dream goddesses Anita Ekberg and Claudia Cardinale.

Italy was cosmopolitan, stylish, European, rich, the place where Ferraris and Alfa Romeos were made. One can see why the Continuous City would seem too stodgy for the moment. Just as the Swedish Amazon Anita Ekberg was the embodiment of desire for Fellini in *La Dolce Vita*, it was

Aerial view, Villaggio Olimpico

Northern European transalpine rationalism, which so terrified Piacentini, that the architects of the Olympic Village seized upon. What could be more anti-Fascist than the very thing Piacentini despised?

The fall of Rome in Piacentini's terms was the Villaggio Olimpico of 1960. Things have never been the same since. The abrupt cultural change you can never find in Edward Gibbon's account of the ancient world did occur in Rome in 1960—a year of total upheaval.

After a generation of resisting the Congress Internationale de la Architecture Moderne (CIAM) and its Athens Charter, Rome suddenly embraced the dogmas of CIAM just as CIAM as an organization imploded. Like Quaroni, the principal architects of Villaggio Olimpico—Adalberto Libera, Luigi Moretti, and Vincenzo Monaco—were ideological acrobats of astonishing agility, swinging from political branch to branch like primates in search of bananas. All had done their best and most famous work in the 1930s under the patronage of Piacentini, but Villaggio Olimpico is about as anti-Roman as architecture can be. It is a conventional Northern European Zeilenbau, straight out of the Athens Charter, consisting of parallel bars of housing, hoisted up on pilotis, completely divorced from streets, and floating in a giant superblock. A couple of the bars are rotated in a feeble, half-hearted attempt at a piazza, but really it is only the color of its brick that makes the slightest reference to the 2,500 years of Roman building.

It is quite a weird place. The Continuous City ends abruptly at its eastern edge, Viale Tiziano, developed in the 1950s as a continuous street of palazzine on their little lots, just like Parioli. Across the street is the large district of the Villaggio, which quite purposely has neither lots nor streets lined with buildings. It is (according to the communist dogma of 1960) an undivided parcel of public land, with a four-lane elevated motorway running down the middle. The centerpiece (if one can use such a hierarchical term for undifferentiated space) is the motorway itself, with an elaborately sculpted substructure by Italy's technological hero of the day, Pier Luigi Nervi. This forlorn, somewhat scary landscape, inhabited only by Nervi's beautiful columns, is the very antithesis of the bustling sociability of a Roman neighborhood. Where is everyone, one wonders on the long trek to nowhere in particular; where can I get a cappuccino or pee?

Roman fabric and Casalino; urbanism as *thing*

Casalino

Casalino, far out on the eastern periphery of the city, is one of the last and largest projects of Ludovico Quaroni, built from 1968 to 1972. I arrived there for my first visit, expecting (and hoping) to detest it, and thereby confirm the thesis of the Continuous City and the Ruptured City.

From drawings and photographs, this high modernist conceit seemed to me like Quaroni's final apostasy as the principal legatee of Marcello Piacentini—anti-Fascism meets Oedipus Rex. Of course, how could Fascism or anti-Fascism be anything more than fashionable clothing to the facile author of both the stupendous Piazza Imperiale at EUR and the folkloric Tiburtino, just a few years apart?

The approach to the site confirms expectations. Though it stands out on the map of Rome—giant bars radiating in a huge fan-shaped thing unto itself—it is almost impossible to find. When one finally gets a glimpse, it is perched on a hill behind a mess of gas stations, auto-repair shops, and the like, finally giving way to a forbidding, forty-foot-high retaining wall made with fancy formwork. So far so good, if one is looking to discredit the Ruptured City.

Then you climb a driveway to a nondescript parking lot, turn left, and there you confront Casalino—and good God, it is so superbly well done it takes your breath away. Ghost of Ludovico Quaroni, I will take back every snide remark, but I don't know what to say to you.

Casalino, the buildings

The almost parallel bars are the ubiquitous *casa in linea* again, this time raised up on *pilotis* in the fashion of transalpine rationalism. The only difference between this and most of the French, German, Swiss, Austrian, and Dutch versions of Zeilenbau social housing is that Quaroni's is really beautiful. On one side of each bar of units there are heroic stair towers, every other unit. On the other side is a syncopated rhythm of deep, well-used balconies. The bars splay slightly and slope slightly, from eight stories on one end of the long bars to four or five on the other. Except for the concrete stair towers, the material throughout is a handsome Roman brick, impeccably detailed.

Between each bar is a beautifully designed and perfectly maintained formal garden. On a level below the gardens is the cleverest, most economical and pleasant solution to a parking podium I have ever seen. The drive aisles of the parking are open to the sky with rows of garages traversed by occasional bridges, and with simple, day-lit little stairs to the gardens above. It is all so straightforward that I blush never to have thought of such a simple and elegant parking solution myself.

One can explain, though perhaps not excuse, the isolated and self-referential nature of Casalino as the product of its time, perhaps of a time slightly earlier than its time. Casalino is what is known as a "167" or *centosesantasiete* project. Law 167 was a key part of Rome's 1962 General Plan, analogous to Title I urban renewal that ripped apart cities in the United States at the same time. It was not a completely new idea, but an extension of what Piacentini wrote into the 1942 modifications of the 1931 General Plan.

Piacentini believed that there should be two tiers of architects—a very few like Giovannoni and himself acting as master planners for large sectors of the city, and a whole cadre of excellent architects such as existed in Rome for individual buildings. Law 167 went further in empowering master architects fully to control large sites, turning projects like Casalino into virtual megastructures or large single buildings stretching for many blocks. Despite his fears, Piacentini probably could never have envisioned a generation of Roman architects swept up in aesthetic and ideological fashion of the times, using their powers as master planners to turn against the heritage of the city. Least of all could he imagine this from his protégé, his Quaroni. But that is what happened.

The spirit of the *boom economico*, Italy's sudden and unprecedented prosperity in the late 1950s, carried well into the 1960s, after the actual growth of the economy had stalled. For a long time Italy was awash in optimism. Italian cars, movies, fashion, products, and style were the envy of the world, and Italians knew it. The grainy black and white of neorealism gave way to the magazine slickness of *La Dolce Vita*. Anna Magnani faded; Anita Ekberg and Claudia Cardinale bloomed. *La Dolce Vita* was a time of hope, and Law 167 was the City of Hope. No looking backward, especially not to the dark days of Fascism and the war, to jackboots, blackshirts, and Marcello Piacentini.

Moreover for Quaroni, there was the desperate question of remaining erect in the crashing surf of the avant-gardist student revolutions of the 1960s, surf that had utterly wiped out his most brilliant colleagues. The ephemeral graphic musings of Super Studio, Archigram, and Archizoom filled the air of architectural schools everywhere, and Quaroni felt the need to at least appear to take them seriously. Even at provincial Berkeley at the farthest edge of Western civilization, my own master's thesis of 1966 was a vast megastructure suffused with a spirit of exhumed futurism.

In the early 1960s, Sapienza students refused their assignment when it consisted of "only" 5,000 housing units. Such a modest program involved fitting into a world that exists, not imagining the world anew. The compulsion to perpetually imagine the world anew is the great neurosis of modernism. Law 167 was the modernist neurosis made operational: zoning for megastructures remaking society in huge pieces. It was promoted by statements such as this one found in an obscure official planning document, as quoted in an academic paper:

The intention of the designers is to create large housing developments autonomous, equipped with all necessary facilities to the functions housing and connected with each other and with the city through an extensive road network with high sliding [sic]. *Following the principles of zoning and planning monofunctional rationalist, imagine residential areas articulated models of morphological and typological free from the strict rules of urbanism nineteenth century, in the rejection of traditional urban design and through the exaltation of the function that determines the shape of the city.*

So what do I say to the ghost of Professore Quoroni? I can tell him that I do understand that all this was in the air, but I am reminded of the question his students put to him in 1958 in regard to Piazza Imperiale:

How could you?

After Casalino, the question is bigger. How could you, who so loved Rome that you produced an encyclopedic history of all of Roman architecture, turn against the city? How could you turn against Rome armed with all your formidable skills, your culture, and your eloquence? Perhaps the ghost of Quaroni would have the same laconic answer for me that he had for his students in 1958:

"I'm good in every style."
From the man who designed Piazza Imperiale, Tiburtino, and Casalino, that remark must rank as a world record in the realm of understatement.

Anagrafe, Rome

Rationalism: What Was Lost?

The radical phase of academic architectural polemic at Sapienza (straddling 1960) despised Piacentini and the architecture of the rationalist period. They labeled it formalistic, formulaic, bound by the shackles of history, and lacking a utopian scale of vision—a list of the worst pejoratives imaginable. Today, if one looks at the incredibly rich legacy of the architecture of the 1920s and '30s in Rome and all over Italy, one can easily argue that those qualities are precisely its strengths. If one looks further at the utterly goofy parametric mannerism that dominates architectural schools today—worse, if one looks at what the few built realities of those fantasies are like—then a formulaic formalism bound by the shackles of history and lacking a utopian scale of vision doesn't sound bad at all.

Italian rationalism, unlike the transalpine version, is the modern architecture of the Continuous City. All over Italy, one sees buildings from the 1920s and '30s, proudly modern buildings, that fit comfortably within and frequently improve the most precious urban settings. Piacentini had some cockeyed planning and racial ideas, but as an architect and leader of an architectural movement, his brilliance is written all over Italy. I am happy to admit that echoes of Italian rationalism appear in my own work, over and over.

Palazzo Poste Telegrafi, Naples; architecture and the city

The two great public building programs of the twentieth century were that of Fascist Italy and America's Works Progress Administration (WPA). Both programs created working-class employment by eschewing labor-saving technology and building with labor-intensive, enduring traditional materials. Stylistically and ideologically, the two programs have many similarities, and both were popular political strategies that lifted their societies from depression.

Three ideas give the rationalist movement its lasting value.

First, it is a consistent formal language of building through which many decent architects did thousands of decent buildings, and a few brilliant architects did masterpieces. In this way, it is like the formal language of the Renaissance, when not everybody was Michelangelo.

Second, rationalist architects had no hesitation about designing individual buildings. They lavished skill and attention on small interventions and sensitive pieces of city repair.

Finally, rationalist buildings are consistently well built out of durable materials that are the same as or compatible with historic buildings. Consider two examples:

It never appears on the A lists of must-sees, but one of my favorite Roman buildings (actually two buildings across the street from one another) is called Anagrafe. Its architect, Ignazio Guidi, had the formidable challenge of designing a huge modern building complex sandwiched among some of Rome's most precious antiquities, the Theater of Marcellus on one side and a little park containing the Tempio di Fortuno and the Tempio di Ercole Vincitore on the other. Anagrafe may not be a masterpiece, but one can marvel at the sheer competence of it—the sure-handed confidence with which Guidi used the well-established common language of material, composition, and robust detail of the rationalist movement to house the repository of birth records for Roman citizens, a celebration of *romanità* with grandeur appropriate to that use and to the magnificence of its neighbors. Guidi knew everything there is to know about inserting a travertine window surround in a brick wall. The Continuous City demands this kind of competence.

The Fascist version of the modern appears nowhere more dramatically or more differently from Northern European modernism than in the heart of Naples. Naples itself is the apotheosis of everything the transalpine rationalist crowd despised about the European city—dirty, congested, noisy, seething with life, totally lacking any sense of rational order, but glorious in its centuries-deep squalid vitality.

Right in the heart of Naples, virtually across the street from its densest, most intensely congested section, the Quartieri Spagnola, is the Piazza Giacomo Matteotti, a typical Italian urban square in all respects, except that it is shaped by and ringed with modern buildings of the highest quality, built in the 1930s. The centerpiece is on the north side of the piazza, the immense convex symmetry of the Palazzo delle Poste e Telegrafici.

The glorification of the postal service and the telegraph system with a monumental building that fully earns the title "palazzo" is part of Fascist propaganda's embrace of technology and the future. The horizontal detailing of curving surfaces and the horizontal glazing of the dramatic three-story lobby entrance convey future-oriented modernity in very much the same decorative language as the great monuments of America's WPA, such as the Hoover Dam or the Golden Gate Bridge. Yet the Palazzo, with the sweep of its tawny stone façade, is like centuries of Roman palazzi, a comfortable resident of the town's historic fabric and a defining element of a traditional Italian piazza.

Meditations on Continuity

In 2015, the Venice Biennale presented two very different views of modern Italian urban history. First was the huge exhibition in the main hall of the Arsenale, entitled *Monditalia*, curated by Rem Koolhaas with many contributors. Second was the much smaller Italian Pavilion curated by Venetian architect Cino Zucchi.

Monditalia was a vast, confusing, and wildly ambitious attempt to document the impact of a century of modernism in Italy. It contained architectural exhibits, a smattering of art, a particularly lame section on modern dance, and forty-two screens showing excerpts from different eras of Italian film. There were probably many ways to read this collage, but what I took from it was a vast lamentation for long-dead dreams of a new society, a deep sadness at the way in which human aspirations, especially the aspirations of architects, are swallowed by history and time. Great buildings built in the glow or afterglow of the postwar *boom economica*, such as Pier Luigi Nervi's Olivetti Factory in Turin, were shown in their current state of abandonment and ruin.

Magnificent Italian rationalist buildings in Libya are shown in their original imperial glory in 1938, and then in their 2009 state of weathered assimilation into the impoverished mess of their surroundings. Accompanying the 1938 images of the great buildings are photographs and descriptions of the vast Italian concentration camps where hundreds of thousands of Libyans perished at Italian hands. Brutal and shocking.

Koolhaas's haunting *Monditalia* exhibit was a deep song of mourning for the City of Hope, or rather two different Italian Cities of Hope—one Fascist, one modernist, separated by thirty years. By contrast, Cino Zucchi's Italian Pavilion was not sad at all. It recorded the work not of the heroic prewar or the prosperous and glamorous postwar, but of contextually sensitive adaptations of urban places over time, and of architecture in the economically weak and politically cynical present. There are no big dreams, but rather a careful, loving appreciation of the best of what exists. All of the new buildings shown were conceived in relation to the particularities of their sites. There is no stylistic consensus, but a rich eclectic pluralism around a general idea that continuity and context are what matters. Much of what was shown is modest and skillful and makes better places. Some of it is beautiful.

Zucchi presented a delicious paradox: that an optimistic future for architecture and society resides in allegiance to the present and repudiation of hope for great days to come; it lies in allegiance to real places as they exist, not to imaginary places as they might be.

In the absence of the City of Hope, in the emptiness of its promises, in the destructive power of hollow dreams, the City of Love seems like the sane and life-affirming alternative. Romans were so good at building the City of Love for so long. It is a joy to study what they did and how they did it, and it is a mystery how these great masters of city building lost their way in their own most cherished of all home towns.

Basketball does not have be the NBA to be interesting. One can be absorbed by a well-played high-school game or even playground pickup. Certainly real baseball fans can appreciate the grace and precision of twelve-year-old infielders turning a Little League double play.

By this principle—that Little League is worth watching—I dare venture out onto the great field of ideas. I have spent upward of 100,000 hours as a working architect. There is no way that I could be a real philosopher or scholar, because the 100,000-hour commitment has simply not left me enough time to read. However, that 100,000-hour experience provides a special vantage point, so while I don't take the field at the same time as Aristotle, Freud, or Oswald Spengler, I do have the temerity to pick up the same ball and bat.

Federico Fellini (left), Martin Heidegger (center), Vladimir Nabokov (right)

CHAPTER 14

Three Giants and a Midget

"Where are you riding, Dolores Haze?
What make is the magic carpet?
Is a Cream Cougar the present craze?
And where are you parked, my car pet?"[1]

—*LOLITA*, VLADIMIR NABOKOV

As far as I know, no one has yet observed that three of the greatest figures of twentieth-century art and thought kept company with the same small, annoying person. The three great men were Federico Fellini, Vladimir Nabokov, and Martin Heidegger, who all spent much of their lives in debate with the same doppelgänger, the same reductive, rationalist nerd who inhabited their minds and whose pesky arguments they spent much of their lives and inner dialogue answering and refuting. From the point of view of city building, this coincidence would not matter much if it were not this same pesky nerd who captured the minds of architects sometime early in the twentieth century. It was he who led them in their rampages against the traditions of urban culture, and who continues to hold many of them in bondage to this day, even reasserting himself as a would-be environmentalist. The pesky nerd is something more menacing than the imaginary playmates that three-year-olds hang out with. He is the sort of demon who inhabits a human form, again and again, sometimes achieving considerable renown, as did the philosopher Rudolph Carnap.

Some explanation is in order. It was probably Fellini who disclosed the identity of the little man and his own struggles with him most clearly. Fellini wrote a part for him in his 1963 autobiographical masterpiece *8½*. The protagonist of *8½* is Guido Anselmi, a film director played by Marcello Mastrionni, then at the peak of his movie star glory. Guido is in crises. He is in the midst of a vast and expensive production, and his muse has deserted him. He is attempting to weave a film around the collage of dreams and memories that haunt him, but, while the entire production company waits, he can think of no link, no rational glue that makes the fractured mosaic in his mind lucid and comprehensible.

Guido's tormentor is his cowriter and designated alter ego, Daumier Carini, played by a singularly unattractive actor named Jean Rougeul, opposite the handsome and infinitely charming Mastrionni. Daumier thinks Guido's script is a mess—meaningless fragments "drowned in nostalgia." Guido's most beguiling fantasy is of a gloriously buxom twenty-three-year-old Claudia Cardinale as a nurse/goddess dressed in white, who appears and reappears as an enigmatic apparition. Carini tells Guido that of all the symbols in his story, "the girl in white is the worst." He tells Guido to get rid of her and to assert "stringent, unassailable logic."

The whole point of *8½* is that Carini doesn't get what is most central and important—the collage of dreams and half memories, of cosmological eroticism and fragmented juxtaposition that constitute the human psyche. Guido is all soul; Carini is a mind without a soul. Guido is the hero; Carini, the fool. In the last great scene of *8½*, all the characters of Guido's memories and fantasies, Claudia Cardinale included, join hands and dance around him in a majestic cosmic game of ring-around-the-rosy, never having found their way into a reductive linear narrative of "stringent, unassailable logic."

Vladimir Nabokov concocts characters like Carini all through his works, sometimes in the guise of "a Viennese quack" (first name Sigmund), whose way of thinking is so arid that he knows nothing of butterflies and cannot converse with children. In his masterful *Ada,* the fool appears first as the imbecile pedant, Dr. Fruit of Signy Mon Dieu Mon Dieu, then as his double, "a Doctor Sig Heiler, whom everybody venerated as a great guy and a near-genius, in the usual sense of near-beer."[2] The demented mother of the hero easily outwits both of the psychiatrist fools on her way to what must be literature's most sane and charming suicide.

At the very beginning of Nabokov's *Lolita*, a psychologist named Dr. Blanche Schwarzmann puts in a brief appearance; her name is a typical Nabokovian multilingual wordplay for one who sees the world only in black and white. Frequently asked about his disdain for Freud and Freudians, he once replied, "Let the credulous and the vulgar continue to believe that all mental woes can be cured by a daily application of old Greek myths to their private parts." Mockery of the little man, his internalized antagonist, was a sport he clearly enjoyed.

Nabokov's Freudians were the most consistently ridiculous of his despised "idea mongers," forever cramming the infinite nuances of human character into a few ugly, prefabricated boxes of arcane terminology, as if no further insight was needed or possible. Nabokov's disdain for reductive thinking was largely aesthetic, for more than anything, he savored the beauty of complex things— orchids, butterflies, human females, and, above all, language. The Edenic world of Ada, so exquisitely described in twentieth-century English's most gorgeous prose, is the lost civilization he watched the Bolshevik brutes destroy. Freud, Lenin, Gropius—he had no use for any of them.

Butterflies were a lifelong obsession for Nabokov, and his pride of accomplishment as a respected lepidopterist equaled his enjoyment of authorial celebrity. Perhaps the pivotal paragraph of his splendid autobiography, *Speak Memory*, concerns butterflies:

When a butterfly has to look like a leaf, not only are all the details of a leaf beautifully rendered but markings imitating grub-bored holes are generously thrown in. "Natural selection" in the Darwinian sense could not explain the miraculous coincidence of imitative aspect and imitative

behavior, nor could one appeal to the "struggle for life" when a protective device was carried to the point of mimetic subtlety, exuberance, and luxury far in excess of a predator's powers of appreciation. I discovered in nature the non-utilitarian delights that I sought in art. Both were a game of intricate enchantment and deception.[3]

Butterflies are not ideologues, and their morphology did not quit when a biological "problem" was "solved." They were never subject to the brute left-brained pragmatism of "value engineering," dreaded by modern-day architects like the torture chambers of the Inquisition. How laden with significance are Nabokov's butterflies for the builders of the modern world and its deprivations? We save our money and vacation days to visit places of "intricate enchantment and deception." We know what they are like and we love them, but in our ideological and epistemological prison, we are forbidden from spending our working days building them except by stealth, or even finding the language to speak of them. Only a few reverent students of magical places even know how.

The modernist triad—Freud, Lenin, Gropius (and you can add to the list)—had not a trace of a quality that Nabokov possessed in abundance—irony and self-mocking wit, accompanied by voracious interest in everything—from Dante and Goethe to Dick Tracy and cowboy westerns. Reductive systematizers—Freudians, logical positivists, modernists—are a leitmotif in the works of Nabokov and Fellini—a recurrent theme, a persistent annoyance, but not the main subject matter of their poetic grandeur.

It was Martin Heidegger, however, who devoted the most concentrated attention to the annoying little fellow. For Heidegger as a young man, it was Descartes who epitomized reductive, arid rationalism, and he devotes long sections of *Being and Time*,[4] the major work of his early career, to the systematic demolition of Cartesian arguments. Keep in mind that Cartesian rationalism is nothing less than the very foundation of modernity, assimilated to the degree that it passes for what we call common sense 200 years later.

Martin Heidegger was a complicated fellow. There is certainly as much to despise about him as there is to admire and revere. He *did* invent a private language of the most awful neologisms (worse in German). He *did* wear lederhosen. And he *was* a Nazi, a relatively unrepentant one. Nonetheless, to some of us in architecture and city building he is a heroic figure, resurrected from obscurity and disgrace by the architectural historian and theorist Christian Norberg-Schulz. It was Heidegger, through Norberg-Schulz, who laid a philosophical foundation for the love of place and the experience of the phenomenon of places. Heidegger's arguments and his strangely invented terminology give rationale and purpose to the places we try to construct and to their antecedents, the places we love. Long before the shortcomings of modernist thinking and the one-dimensional city of the slab block became so vividly manifest in the world, Heidegger laid bare its idiocy.

Heidegger begins his demolition derby of Cartesian rationalism with Descartes's first premise: I think, therefore I am. Heidegger considers this a fundamentally backward proposition. It imagines human subjects fully formed, floating around on three-dimensional graph paper, bumping now and then into mute, brute objects that constitute the external world and that have nothing to do with the making of the thinking subject in the first place. In this rational land of objects on graph paper (so like the modernist city), epistemology (knowledge) precedes ontology (being). For Heidegger, by contrast, people and their worlds are inseparable, and thinking before being—the subject/object dualism that underlies most of what we call modernity—is nonsense.

Exactly as Le Corbusier intended, the modernist city is a literal translation of the Cartesian universe into a built reality, a constructed metaphor of vast and terrifying dimensions. The Heideggerian conception of "place" was conceived by Norberg-Schulz and others in opposition to the Cartesian idea of "space," which underlies every stick of modern architecture and modernist town planning. The slab block or Zeilenbau occupies and defines that very form of Cartesian space.

It is a crucial part of the story of the modernist city that Le Corbusier chose the term "Cartesian" to describe the skyscraper and slab-block landscape of his imagination, the landscape that became the dogma of CIAM and the built reality of so much of the modern world. What Le Corbusier meant by the evocation of Descartes was that these buildings would be the perfect embodiment of rational thought, standing free and unfettered in a matrix of undifferentiated space. They would ignore and ultimately eradicate the messy, irrational layering of centuries that burdened cities and distorted their architecture.

Being and Time dismantles the narrow and impoverished Cartesian view of the world, a view that in Heideggerian terms "unworlds the world" and tries to drain things of all the meaning they have for us. For Heidegger, full-fledged space consists not of the arid universe of the x, y, and z Cartesian coordinates with disembodied objects floating around among them, but of places of myth and history, where people belong and dwell, and where things matter because they are laden with meaning. We are the worlds we inhabit, not dispassionate observers of mute externalities. They make us as surely as we make them; we don't exist without them or before them.

A Heideggerian "world" is the amniotic fluid of history, myth, and experience that we are formed within. Heidegger is a contextualist in a sense that is deeper and more evocative than the much more literal way architects normally use the word. The layers of history are a predicating condition for existence. An erased world, a ruptured world, is an oxymoron; it is not a world at all. A city, therefore, is a Heideggerian world, not unlike the world of a Fellini film. In fact, cities are the subject matter of many of Fellini's best films, either the Ravenna of his youth (*I Vitteloni*) or Rome (*The White Sheik*, *La Dolce Vita*, *8½*, *Roma*). For Fellini, Ravenna and Rome were the repositories of myth and memory, indelible and irreducible. If that renders them enigmatic and incomprehensible, that is quite all right.

For most of the last half of the twentieth century, including the time when Fellini and Nabokov did their work, Heidegger was dismissed in the English-speaking world as a charlatan and a fake. Rudolph Carnap was the leader of the logical positivists in the 1930s, the ultimate Cartesian rationalist, the real guy of whom Fellini's Daumier Carini was the parody. He denounced Heidegger's writing as a dangerously confused concoction, not worth reading. And largely because of Carnap, it wasn't. Following Carnap's lead, Bertrand Russell, no less, called Heidegger's writings "language run riot."

Today the builders of cities—architects and town planners—are pressed to find or create convincing metrics (the word of the hour) to compete in the quest for the Sustainable City. Reductive positivism, the tyranny of empiricism, is with us as never before. We live in an era of rating systems, points, and prerequisites, of universal codes and prescriptions, of measures that measure the measurable but will never measure the culture of the city, its most precious and fragile content and legacy. In this context, Christian Norberg-Shulz's retrieval of Heidegger from academic banishment, his use of Heidegger to anchor an alternative to the arid graph paper city of numbers promulgated in the name of modernity, seems more important and timely than ever. Perhaps he can lead us once more out from the dark shadows of Carnap.

The very name "Professor Carnap" sounds like a coinage from Nabokov, like Lolita's full name—Dolores Haze, the mists of sadness. The name Carnap could denote the essential characteristic of the century we recently lived through, something soporific about our chosen way of getting about, going to sleep on the back seat and forgetting the myths and history of our urban culture as the car runs rampant over it all, as it propels us through the graph paper universe of the modernist city or the ravaged landscape of sprawl.

> *Magic carpet, car pet, carnap.*
> *Wake up, little Susy;*
> *The carnap is over.*

The fact is that my three giants all are dependent on their Carnapian doppelgänger. They all define themselves principally in relation to him; he an integral and necessary part of their being; they are much less without him.

The three giants are giants because they didn't surrender to the little man as much of modernity has. They are refusniks in the epistemological plea bargain that modern times have made with technology; they have stayed out of its cognitive gulag. It is not as if empirical pragmatism has ever gone away or ever will. How could one possibly function as a working architect without a highly developed inner streak of Carnap? For that matter, how could one function as a working anything but a shaman or an artist? The three giants lived by the principle that, while we must spend time in the Cartesian city, it is not our home; we actually dwell in the labyrinthine lanes, passages, and alleys of myth, memory, and history,

The three giants are part of a small but splendid chorus that includes the great explorer and explainer of the human soul, neurologist, and essayist Oliver Sacks, and Charles Eisenstein, author of the colossal tome *The Ascent of Humanity*.[5] They join the three giants as conspirators plotting strategy of escape from the mechanistic paradigm that has produced, among other things, the City of Hope. For Sacks, a component of that spiritually blind machine is conventional organic neurology, which sees the human mind as a mechanism that is either functioning "correctly" or suffering from "deficits" in the form of broken parts.[6] Sacks sees many of those deficits as rich and worthy aspects of the human.

Eisenstein contributes a vivid and beautiful metaphor to the argument. He sees Cartesian rationalism as the primal human campfire, its light converting the unknown into the known, and providing within its circle the comforting companionship of the certain. Like the campfire, however, it deepens the shadows of the vastness beyond its circle of light, makes it so impenetrable that those closest to fire can deny its existence altogether.

CHAPTER 15

Whatever Happened to Modernity?

Ideas seep through unseen fissures; they drip and form big puddles and ponds. One can drown in such a pond and have no sense of where it came from. Architects, who may tend to be more passionate than reflective, seem susceptible to immersion in beliefs that come from places unknown to them. But sometimes one can search the cracks and actually find the source from which the puddles and dangerous ponds emanated.

Because of its extraordinary influence, the Graduate School of Design at Harvard is a good place to hunt for such seepages. And within the GSD, what better place to look than the syllabus of the first-year theory class required of all incoming students. What one finds is very strange.

In the course syllabus as frequently taught by Professor Michael Hayes, assignment one, week one, is to read a substantial excerpt from *Space, Time and Architecture* by Harvard architecture's original court historian, Sigfried Giedion. The thesis of *Space, Time and Architecture*[1] goes something like this: The way people see and perceive things changes with the times. As evidence, Giedion invokes the standard art-historical view of the relationship between Renaissance humanism and the discovery of the laws of perspective. He then claims a similar relationship among a series of modern phenomena, including the theory of relativity, cubism, steel frame construction, and high-speed transportation. The term space/time is his shorthand for a modern revolution in the perception of architecture and cities, equivalent to the discovery of perspective.

It is safe to say that most contemporary architectural historians now regard *Space, Time and Architecture* as pseudohistory and ingenious period-piece propaganda. Perhaps to insulate his students from this heretical view, Professor Hayes tells his fledglings how to read Giedion by providing in the syllabus a handy "Premise for Interpreting Giedion."

. . . modern architecture plays a significant role in an ongoing cognitive revolution—that extended process of intellectual transformation whereby a society whose life habits and perceptual apparatuses were formed by other, now anachronistic, modes of production are effectively reprogrammed for life in the new industrialized world.

To paraphrase Professor Hayes's paraphrase of Giedion in simpler words, he is saying that if people don't like the mechanization and abstraction of our brand of modern architecture, don't worry; it's their fault. As a properly trained modern architect and an initiate into the true workings of historical process, you have an obligation not to listen to them. Instead you should work hard to "reprogram" them, Maoist fashion.

Right after Giedion in the syllabus, now into the second week of graduate school, comes an introduction to the Frankfurt School for Social Research, with special emphasis on (of all things) Theodor Adorno and his *Philosophy of Modern Music*,[2] published in its final form in 1949. If Giedion is the foundation for a system of ideas, Adorno is the keystone. Generations of GSD graduates recall their encounter with Adorno.

The thrust of this essay is to compare and contrast false modernity and true modernity, represented respectively by the music of Igor Stravinsky and Arnold Schoenberg. For Adorno, Stravinsky was the prisoner of historical sentiment, his music filled with references to folk tunes, primitivism, marches, and classical structure. Schoenberg, on the other hand, was the true adventurer in the modern spirit, since his twelve-tone system is a pure abstraction, an invention of the mind incapable of reference to anything outside itself. Reading this text at the very beginning of architecture school lends gravitas to the idea that true modern buildings also should have no reference to things outside themselves, including the cities of which they are part. Professor Hayes carefully lays the foundation for the ruptured city, the city of erasure, and slab-block modernism in week two.

What's more, Adorno argues that Schoenberg's harsh dissonances are an appropriate art for the harsh, dissonant turmoil of modern life as opposed to Stravinsky's "neo-classical objectivism," a construct of what he called "premature harmonies, ignoring the persistence of social contradictions." May God spare first-year architecture students from suffering "premature harmonies."

In his book *The Dialectical Imagination*, the great Berkeley scholar Martin Jay has observed that most of the Marxist intellectuals of the Frankfurt School, like Karl Marx himself, were Jewish.[3] Though they were assimilated and secular, they retained an element of Jewishness in their thinking, and they freely appropriated the Jewish doctrine of the Messiah, giving it a new name— *the Revolution*. Until the revolution comes, society will remain in a fundamental state of disorder. The function of art is to reify or give expression to this state of disorder and thereby raise social consciousness and hasten the revolution. Therefore all worthy art must have an element of negativism or dissonance about it. Art that does not suffers from "premature harmonies." Sorry everyone, no joy allowed until after the revolution.

One of the forms of "premature harmony" that Adorno attacked most viciously was American jazz, which he pronounced "yatz" and associated with the German word "hatz," a pejorative for the baying of a bloodhound. He wrote the long, vituperative essay "On Jazz" in 1933, never having heard any jazz in live performance, but continued revising the essay and making it even nastier after he came to this country in 1940. In jazz, he saw American Negroes as complicit in their own oppression. An unrepentant Eurocentric, he dismissed the jazz of the 1950s as watered-down Delius and Debussy—but he found one thing positive (that is, in Marxist terms—negative) in the lead instrument of 1950s bebop—the saxophone. He observed that the saxophone is a metal horn played like a woodwind. It therefore has a kind of sexual ambiguity or *zwischengeschechtlichkeit*, and since this androgyny represents a critical challenge to the established sexual order of society, the saxophone is okay.

In their second week at Harvard's Graduate School of Design, newly minted architecture students are taken on this through-the-looking-glass journey into the topsy-turvy world of Marxist aesthetic theory, where positive is negative, negative is positive, and the redeeming quality of a saxophone is its androgyny. In fairness to Professor Hayes, his course goes on to present other contending points of view, and some, such as those of Robert Venturi and Colin Rowe, are more congenial to architecture's role in urbanism. But these later readings are a bit like comparative religion as taught at Notre Dame, unlikely to win large numbers of converts to Islam or Buddhism.

The institution has a point of view, and Professor Hayes's message to fledgling architects at Harvard (and to those unfortunates consigned to be elsewhere) is clear enough: populist hostility to an abstract modernism is philistine ignorance and should be ignored; references to vernacular building, the imperatives of place or classicism, are inadmissible; and dissonance, not harmony, is the order of the day. By the second week of school, the seeds of hostility to an architecture of place, context, historical continuity, and city building are well sown at Harvard.

If Michael Hayes's tune has a familiar ring, it is because you could never listen to a Charlie Rose interview of a star architect without hearing echoes of it. These ideas pervade architectural culture, whether or not those who believe in them have any idea of their source. From the studiously unpretentious language of Frank Gehry to its opposite in the many big words of Peter Eisenman, what unites the purveyors of the blobs to those of the wiggles and the shards is a set of ideas that come from Sigfried Giedion and Theodor Adorno out of Michael Hayes.

The Hegelian view of history says that revolutions breed counterrevolutions of equal and opposite force. If this is true, it explains why, after seventy years of the modernist hegemony and versions of the Harvard curriculum in most architecture schools, an institution like the Institute for Classical Architecture should appear on the American scene and flourish with some vigor.

ICA events are typically about a fabulous collection of Dresden porcelain, or a tour of a 200-room mansion owned by Doris Duke or someone like her on a thousand-acre estate in Santa Barbara or Newport or somewhere similar. The ICA's biggest event of the year, its Oscar night, is the annual Driehaus Awards dinner.

When I attended in 2005, it was held in a downtown Chicago high-rise. Thanks to American building technology of the 1920s, this was the largest perpendicular Gothic interior I've ever seen, next to Westminster Abbey, twice the size of any similar room at Cambridge or Oxford. There was a sprinkling of people I knew, but mostly it was a big crowd of surprisingly young strangers. I later learned that the youngest of the young were actually Notre Dame architecture students attending on assignment. The young women—whatever their talents, accomplishments, and politics—were absolutely radiant with a fragrant, pre-Raphaelite innocence that I thought had been expunged from the world forever by Coco Chanel and her generation twenty years before I was born. Astonishingly for an architectural gathering, there was not an unstructured black jacket in sight. Except for the conspicuously frumpy presence of the Congress for the New Urbanism board, the hundreds of mostly young men seemed to frequent the same excellent tailor as Prince Charles. Where in the world, I wondered, do these people *shop*?

The highlight of the evening was the awarding of the Driehaus prize to the English neoclassical architect Quinlan Terry. He accepted the award and said the following:

We must build in the manner of our forefathers, in brick and lime masonry. If we do so, the natural orders of architecture will reemerge: the Doric, the Ionic, and the Corinthian.

He said this with a straight face to enthusiastic applause while standing on the twenty-second floor of a skyscraper, surrounded by the architectural treasures of the Chicago loop, from William Lebaron Jenny and Louis Sullivan to Frank Gehry's Pritzker Pavilion across the street, surely one of the great public spaces in America. That this skillful and intelligent architect, Quinlan Terry, neither saw nor acknowledged any of that was clearly a matter of choice. It is the same choice to resist assimilation into the larger culture for the sake of traditional values that the Hassidic Jews of Brooklyn make. It is a choice that is perfectly okay for an architect, like a musician joining an early music consort, but it is not a choice for city builders. The city is inexorably engaged with its own history, and the gears of history, like a good bicycle, have many speeds forward, but, like a bicycle, no reverse.

Many people think that all New Urbanists are just like Quinlan Terry, trying to ride their bicycles backward, and like him, unwilling to engage with the real culture around us. What is around us are the forces of technological change, population pressure, environmental degradation, global warming, hegemonic urban sprawl. The Driehaus Awards dinner was a gathering of a committed subculture, which is attractive to some young people, but I think not very many.

Where do the others go and why?

Most of them do not choose to decontextualize their own lives; in fact, they regard being plugged in to the way things are going as a high virtue. It is a reason New Urbanism has been so coldly shunned in academia. We can thank Rem Koolhaas and his graphic designer, Bruce Mau, for the book *Content*,[4] which defines the very look of "with it" and contextualizes the work of town planners and architects in current events with special vividness. They portray the dark side of globalization with terrifying diagrams that show how China's brutal sweat-shop economy has sucked the economic life out of Europe and the US. Koolhaas puts his dark insights about the world and his own work right on the cover of the book—"Big Brother Skyscrapers," "Sweat Shop Demographics." With glee, he casts himself in the role of Prince of Darkness, according to his own vision of hell. He records for our amusement some light-hearted banter with Prada *fashionistas* about the desperate poverty of Lagos, and he sneaks in some Larry Flynt–style photographs of female genitalia. Naughty, naughty, I guess is the point, in the modernist tradition of provocative mischief.

Credit Koolhaas for extending the limits of provocative mischief beyond any previous limits. His design for the CCTV Building in Beijing is a dazzling symbol, but it is a symbol of state oppression; in fact, it is literally the very instrument of oppression. CCTV's control of information is more vast and insidious than that of Google, which eradicated the existence of Tiananmen Square's heroic Tank Man from the internet as accessed from China.

Imagine a situation in which 97 percent of the residential fabric of New York and Chicago, including the most vibrant neighborhoods, were demolished in ten years, and the population was forcibly relocated to sterile new suburbs through a massively corrupt system of expropriation. Imagine that occurring with the television, press, and an internet police force forbidding any murmur of protest. Without any exaggeration, that is exactly the case in Shanghai and Beijing today, and it is what the CCTV building celebrates.

To achieve the symbolic and terrifying about-to-topple cantilever of the CCTV building, Koolhaas enlisted ARUP Engineers. In a little essay he calls "Post-modern Engineering," he discusses how ARUP used its computational might to analyze the indeterminate redundancies and concentrations of loads and thereby derive the irregular patterns of the trusses that hold up the monstrous cantilever. He wonders what happened to the engineer's creed of scientific rationalism that would have been revolted by the exercise, and asks wistfully, "Why don't they just say NO?"

Again the rhythms of Winston Churchill during the fearful days of 1940 come to mind . . . *a new dark age made more protracted and sinister by the likes of perverted science.*[5]

In a strange turnaround, *avant-gardeism* has found steady employment as an agent of the dark side of globalization. Do not think for a minute that Rem Koolhaas's CCTV is an aberrant exception in this regard.

In 2006, New York's Museum of Modern Art mounted an exhibition titled *On-Site*, celebrating what then curator Terrance Reilly considered the vitality of new architecture in Spain. A large portion of the show was new social housing, all of it autonomous slab-monster buildings far off on the urban fringe, with no reference to surroundings, history, or daily life. These are places for the Spanish to stash their Algerians, Turks, Africans, and Arabs. In a compositionally conceived, giant windblown hole on the twelfth floor of one such block is daycare space for the next generation of truck bombers. As disputes over immigration policy tear at the social fabric of Europe, architecture honored by MoMA does its large part to ensure that these immigrant populations will never assimilate into European life. They will remain isolated, hateful, and hated.

The social housing in *On-Site* is exactly the opposite of what New Urbanists were able to accomplish through HUD's HOPE VI and its successor programs, where immigrant populations

Social housing, Madrid; celebrated by MoMA

and our own poor are integrated into classic American neighborhoods. One can't claim that everything HOPE VI produced lives up to its intentions, but the intentions are unimpeachable: to use the continuity of the city and its architectural traditions to heal rather than inflame the latent schisms of race and class. HOPE VI was where the aesthetically conservative strain of New Urbanism found a high social purpose.

But the New Urbanist movement finds itself in a loony situation. On one hand there is a powerful modernist establishment comprising the best universities, museums throughout the world, the professional architectural press, and most (not all) journalistic critics. For them, town building and architecture are history-less and apolitical subjects. Reference to anything prior to the modern period is culturally inadmissible, and belief in social purpose is just not hip. There are, of course, exceptions to this, but not many and not with vigorous voice.

On the other hand, opposing the modernist juggernaut is this now-thriving revivalist movement that does little to dispel the impression that it is willfully oblivious to the technical, demographic, and political changes that distinguish our time from other times.

Environmentalism has made some inroads into these patterns of self-marginalization, but only a little. We all stand in the cross-fire of a self-referential, socially disengaged modernity on one hand, and on the other, a revival of classical knowledge that has so far failed to separate itself from a longing for the riding-to-the-hounds society that was eradicated in WWI.

It is worth taking a somewhat wayward journey outside the boundaries of architecture and town planning to visit three more cultural giants who seem to point the way around this apparently intractable and menacing cultural schism.

Let's begin with Coco Chanel, couturier and entrepreneur extraordinaire.

Consider a quintessential modernist object—the supremely beautiful, elegant, and unchanging seventy-five-year-old design for the bottle of Chanel No. 5. At first glance this design appears to confirm Theodor Adorno's conception of the modern, its abstraction and rejection of narrative reference. Before Chanel No. 5, perfumes had names such as Night in China, Harem Musk, or Dark Fantasy. The bottle rejects all that in favor of an abstraction, a bit of pseudoscience implying the formulation and testing of Chanel's 1 through 4, which probably never existed, and also love for the beautiful form of the Helvetica "No. 5." But Chanel was not selling perfume bottles; she was selling perfume. Perfume is all about sexuality, and smell—the most animal of the senses, packaged in a bottle. It is the abstraction of the bottle that makes the sensuality of the contents all the more vivid and meaningful.

The bottle of Chanel No. 5 is like Chanel's clothing and like her life, a splendid contradiction and a seamless synthesis of opposites. She was not only the most original, gifted, and prolific designer of her generation, she was a business genius on the scale of an Andrew Carnegie. She started in a foundling home, absolutely penniless, and built an industrial empire, all of her own conception, the first and probably history's most powerful woman CEO. But she never concealed or was in the least embarrassed by the fact that she began her career as a demimondaine whose rich lovers competed for her sexual favors with gobs of money to back her first ventures.

Karl Lagerfeld, the current director of the House of Chanel, says splendidly, *Chanel was a mystery and a paradox. Reality is bearable only if it is made up of such things.*[6]

In her cosmos it was inconceivable that femininity and feminism could be considered different ideas. She wanted to dress a woman so that she could enter a room on equal terms with the general, the bishop, and the head of state, as confident and reassured by her dress as they were. Her version of femininity was simultaneously egalitarian and aristocratic, athletic and erotic. She dressed as a woman to go the opening of the Paris Opera in a way that you knew she was capable

of climbing a tree. She believed in physical ease as the predicating condition for elegance. She referred to classical antiquity in clothing made of industrial mass-produced fabrics such as jersey, and she absolutely mastered the traditional crafts of the milliner and tailor. The October 1926 *Vogue* called her classic "little black dress" the "Chanel Ford, the frock that all the world will wear." In Chanel's cosmology, there are no schisms, no ruptures, no opposition of history and modernity; nothing schizophrenic or contradictory in the combination of her artistry, her capitalist zeal, and her sexuality.

Chanel classics

Chanel's two main ideas—her conception of women and her idea of the relationship of abstraction to life—are completely congruent with those of her friend and collaborator, George Balanchine, the second and perhaps the biggest figure on my list. It is not overstating the case to say that Balanchine's choreography united a classical tradition and modernism with more originality, force, and enduring success than any other artist in any discipline. In this regard, his work, his contribution, and his life story are one and the same. If one tries to draw lessons from the synthesis he brought about, it is worth knowing how Balanchine became Balanchine, because his story is as rich with contradictions as Chanel's. He too was something of a mystery and a paradox, and he liked it that way.

His career began at age ten when he was accepted into the Imperial Ballet School in St Petersburg, a part of the court of Tsar Nicholas II. In the Frenchified court of the tsars, classical ballet, which evolved from fencing exercises in the court of Louis XIV, was preserved and perfected. Before ballet was a professional performing art, it was an essential component of court etiquette—geometric, neo-Platonic perfection applied to the body. Balanchine was raised at court, often appearing as a teenager in the fabled Mariinsky Theater with its greatest stars.

After the tumult of WWI and the Russian Revolution, he found himself, age twenty-one, undernourished and unemployed in Paris with a small group of young Mariinsky dancers. Then fatefully, the twentieth century's greatest genius at recognizing genius, Serge Diaghilev, invited him to audition. Diaghilev audaciously made this superbly trained classical dancer, and the most supremely elegant of all twenty-one-year-olds, the ballet master of his world-famous Ballets Russes. His first assignment was to collaborate with Igor Stravinsky and Henri Matisse, no less, on reworking of the ballet *Le Chant du Rossignol*. Matisse did the sets, costumes, and makeup and arranged red and white chrysanthemums in the hair of the principal ballerina, Alicia Makarova. Coco Chanel hosted the cast party after the opening and Stravinsky played the piano at the party.

The other Ballets Russes artists that young Balanchine was thrown in with included Picasso, Prokofiev, Tchelitchew, Jean Cocteau, Kurt Weill, Lotte Lenya—an unbelievable list. He went from the court of Nicholas II to Diaghilev's court of modernism at its absolute pinnacle of excellence.

Professor Michael Hayes begins the education of architects with Adorno's sour diatribe against Stravinsky, and it is revealing that Stravinsky found his natural collaborator, George Balanchine, in the most sensual of the arts—ballet. Just like the bottle of Chanel No. 5, the most characteristic and famous of the Stravinsky/Balanchine ballets strip away all narrative reference: no storytelling and no sets, costumes that refer only to the dancer's bodies. In the most famous Balanchine/Stravinsky collaborations, dancers in skintight black-and-white practice clothes are etched against a brilliant blue, featureless background. There is nothing on the stage but the life force of the music and the geometries he makes of the dancers themselves. And Balanchine's dancers were better schooled in classical dance, more disciplined than any dance company had been before. Balanchine's grand abstractions demanded more from the corps de ballet than had ever been asked of it—more athleticism, musicality, speed, articulated precision of steps.

When his vision exceeded what even his own superbly trained corps could do, he would arrange his soloists or principal dancers in formation and use them like a chess master attacking with his bishops. Balanchine was a modernist who extended the tradition of classicism he inherited. He was also a modernist who was not a slave to modernity. He carried the whole history of ballet in his head and did all kinds of things with it. Narrative story ballets, huge spectacle ballets, Broadway musical comedy that he revolutionized, and movies.

Balanchine shared a distinctive trait of character with heroes of the previous chapter, Vladimir Nabokov and Federico Fellini. They were all witty in the same ironic way, and they all despised and mocked theorizing. When asked what a performance was about, Balanchine replied "about twenty-eight minutes." [7] They left grand statements of principle to the people Nabokov derisively

Balanchine *Corps de Ballet*

called "idea mongers." As artists who lived through the Russian Revolution and Fascism, their mistrust of idea mongers was at the center of their being. Sigmund Freud and Walter Gropius were not their kind of guys. Unlike them, Balanchine managed to be modernist without being an ideologue or a prig.

Over their long careers, Stravinsky and Balanchine managed a trick that architects and town planners should be able to do, and one that is strictly forbidden in the diktat of Harvard aesthetic theory. They were able to engage popular culture on its own terms, excel within it, and never compromise their own standards. When things got slow in 1941, Balanchine even took a job with Ringling Bros. choreographing elephants. He asked Stravinsky to collaborate with him, and Stravinsky had only one question: Would the elephants be young? Balanchine assured him that they would be young and beautiful and the collaboration proceeded.

As I began this text, I thought the third hero of this chapter would be the founder and director of Jazz at Lincoln Center, Wynton Marsalis. An instrumentalist, he shifts from the music of Joseph Hayden to Jelly Roll Morton to John Coltrane with the same authority and fluency as Balanchine, and Jazz at Lincoln Center is surely one of America's great ecumenical cultural institutions.

I called my very learned jazz musician and composer friend Pat Gleeson to ask him what he thought of this. He said, "No, no, no, not Wynton. He's a very good musician, he's a really good composer, he's a great teacher, but he is absolutely not the Balanchine of jazz. Duke Ellington is the Balanchine of jazz. Wynton is a giant, but he is a conservative and divisive force in American music. For him, Ornette Coleman doesn't exist, Miles Davis and Herbie Hancock are apostates, and rock and roll and hip hop are worthless junk. He is to jazz what that friend of yours in Florida is to New Urbanism. Let me write you some notes about Duke Ellington."

I didn't quite agree with all this, but I understood his point.

The next day I received a brilliant emailed text in praise of Duke Ellington—much too long, dense, and technical to paraphrase. It included references to rhythmic structures and chromatics, Rachmaninoff and Tchaikovsky, blues, W. C. Handy, Ethyl Waters, European royalty, a gut-bucket novelty tune called *Ducky Whackey*, movie scores, Harlem drug addicts, Scriabin and Milhaud, low-life, high-life, and everything in between. Pat convinced me that Duke Ellington should be hero number three. In its complexity, elegance, accessibility, the catholicity of its sources, and its enduring power, the music of Duke Ellington stands proudly beside the works of the other giants of this text.

These three people were such complete masters of their disciplines that they could draw upon its entire history as situations demanded. None of them were ever prevented from doing anything that interested them by an ideology or an aesthetic canon that made some things off limits.

A question to ask then is, Were there ever people in the worlds of urbanism and architecture who were as cosmopolitan, brilliantly free of dogma, eclectic, simultaneously modern, and embracing of history as Chanel, Balanchine, and Ellington?

Duke Ellington

The fact is that modernity as a driving force in architecture and town planning predates the intellectual and stylistic rigidities of Harvard/MoMA/CIAM modernism by half a century at least. During that long span of time there were classically trained architects in many places, fascinated by implications of new technologies and the problems and possibilities of the new industrial city. Cities and city dwellers suffered in many ways from the 1850s through the 1920s, but one thing those cities and city dwellers did not suffer from during those years was the systematic unlearning of their historic craft by architects and builders. That triumph of dogma over knowledge and culture came later.

Ultimately, modernity's answers to the problems of the nineteenth-century industrial city were the city of sprawl and city of erasure, and their joint offspring, the autonomous slab block. The argument of these essays is that those were bad answers to old problems, and they are worse answers to today's problems. Yet they are still around, still with their champions, still clamoring for relevance.

The spirit of modernity did not always align itself with the rupture of the city and its history. There is a long list of architects during the period of 1850 to 1920, protomodern times, who were cosmopolitan eclectics in a way that seems appropriate as role models for urban architects of the twenty-first century. Of this list, one who stands out as most gifted and interesting is Austrian Otto Wagner, architect to Franz Joseph, the last Hapsburg emperor. He, perhaps more than any other, represented the contribution that architecture should make to urbanism, and, as a teacher, what architectural training should consist of, so that generations of architects can contribute to urbanism as the city conditions change.

Wagner was a schooled classicist who consciously placed himself in competition with Michelangelo, Palladio, and Bernini, without copying them directly. But he considered it his mission as an architect and teacher to move from classicism to a modern *nutzstil*—a classically based negation of literal revivalism that espoused appropriate expression of the programs and building methods of the times. He was fascinated both by the spatial order of the traditional city and the new systems of the industrial city. His urban bridges and metro stations are among the most beautiful works of public infrastructure ever conceived. He mastered the decorative language of classicism but experimented relentlessly with the formal possibilities of new materials and fabrication techniques. With more flamboyance than anyone, he dared to use Jugendstil ornament at the scale of urban buildings. The scope of his genius is best expressed through his evolution of aerial perspective drawing—exquisite watercolors that show simultaneously the spatial order of the future city and its relationship to its transportation infrastructure, natural setting, and the formal character of buildings.

Urban infrastructure, Otto Wagner

Otto Wagner, architect to the emperor, died of starvation and influenza in 1918, seven weeks before the armistice. The collapse of the Austro-Hungarian Empire brought about a completely new political and economic situation in Vienna, and it was Wagner's pupils, the *Wagnerschuler*, who had exactly the right skills to adapt and build magnificently in the new Marxist/Leninist Viennese social democracy that emerged in the ruins.

Eve Blau's splendid book *The Architecture of Red Vienna*[8] tells this story. After the Great War, the new socialist government controlled only the historic city center and not its surrounding countryside, and it confronted an urgent need to house a large, dispossessed urban proletariat. They had to be housed quickly and economically in the midst of the remaining glories of the baroque imperial city—but in a way that celebrated their status as the backbone of the new economy and political regime.

Who better than the *Wagnerschuler* to bring about this synthesis of new circumstance and the historic city? German and Dutch experiments with the Zeilenbau or slab-block modernism also began shortly after WWI. But that form of systematic social housing was completely unsuited to the circumstance of Vienna. Vienna did not control enough land to sprawl, and the historic city was too intact and valuable to erase. Vienna had to be a regenerated Continuous City; there was no other choice. If for many reasons, the Continuous City is the only choice for the sustainable city of the twenty-first century, Vienna of the period 1919 to 1933 is worth study.

Red Vienna versus German housing and town planning of same period was the first bout in a long series of matches and rematches between the slab block and perimeter block. Through the 1920s, the Zeilenbau, or slab block, evolved toward its highest state of abstract refinement in the works of Ernst May. At the same time, Viennese architects developed its antitype, the *Gemeindebau*, a pattern of perimeter block suitable for irregular infill sites in the existing city. The never-hermetic *Gemeindebau* embraced and connected to the historic fabric around it, and through grand portals in its perimeter connected surrounding streets to networks of courtyards that housed the social services, health facilities, gyms, and communal gardens that were symbols of the new socialist state. To this day, the social housing of Red Vienna is one of the glories of the world and represents a synthesis, never equaled, of classical architectural principles, urbanism, and the modern spirit.

Gemeindebau woven into the city

The architecture of Red Vienna put in a brief appearance in the United States. The 1920s garden apartment movement in New York reached its apogee in a series of social housing projects in the Bronx, sponsored by garment workers' unions for their members. The planning, programming, and decorative language of these enduringly beautiful buildings are straight out of Red Vienna, and even today they are some of the most livable dwellings in the city. Abruptly, however, the garden apartment movement came to an end as the rival form of Euro-modernism seized the stage in the early 1930s. The Gropius, Adorno, Giedion, abstract, systematic, slab-block hegemony took center stage, while the subtle and adaptable urban perimeter block was chased from the academy and the museums to various less exalted realms.

Simultaneously, the architecture of Red Vienna itself came to an even more abrupt and symbolic end in 1934 with the routing of the socialist administration and the shelling of the most famous icon of Red Vienna, Karl Marx Hof, by right-wing militias called the *Heimwehr*.

It is significant that the *Wagnerschule* ethos was eradicated by the same cultural forces that have swirled around the New Urbanist movement and marginalized it from academic studies, if not from the practice of building, where it survives mostly in coarse and corrupted form. In Europe, the spirit of the *Wagnerschule* was wiped out by neoclassicism from the Right in Germany and Austria, and by the adoption of conservative vernacular in the form of *heimatstil* by the Nazis. In America the cultural wipeout was at the hands of hegemonic modernism, emanating first from the Museum of Modern Art and slightly later from Harvard.

What is fascinating and important is that at the same time this cultural wipeout was occurring with respect to architecture and the city, the very same attitude that the *Wagnerschuler* embodied was flourishing in other art forms and is still flourishing to this day. That is what the list of cultural giants is about; it is why they should be interesting and relevant to architects and twenty-first-century urbanists. The attitude that unites them consists of a fascination with what is new in the moment one is living through, and simultaneous reverence for the historical past of one's discipline; fidelity to the highest standards of excellence and an absence of dogma—a playful eclecticism that allows one to do many things and perform in many situations.

The Charter for the New Urbanism, LEED, and LEED-ND (LEED for Neighborhood Development) may get a city builder off on the right foot, but then comes the terrifying moment when an architect, urbanist, or environmentalist must actually build something that satisfies all the different dimensions of scrutiny with which we experience the world. At this point you must leave the solid ground of dogma, principles, and positivistic method and soar like the giants on the gossamer wings of skill, taste, and the imagination or crash into the ground. This breathless moment—soar or crash—is the crux of it. Reducing it to the formulaic or the measured will never do. The giants never did.

The subject of urbanism is place-making. It is about place-making in a complicated world in which many forces are unleashed to rob places of their distinctiveness, meaning, and sustaining power over the quality of our lives. The infinite nuances of place demand from a maker of place suppleness, mastery of craft, and adaptability that the modernist hegemony systematically eliminated from architectural training. It also demands alertness to what is going on in the world and ability to cope with its ruthless pressures.

For an urban architecture to succeed, to serve the twenty-first-century city and endure as Balanchine's influence has so brilliantly, it must embrace architectural literacy, but it cannot be an architectural style. To be a maker of place, one must climb trees and dress for the opera, play the music of King Frederick the Great and King Oliver with equal fluency, and be able to enjoy choreographing elephants. Otto Wagner did all those things just fine. Some of us are trying our best.

CHAPTER 16

Meet a Force of History

One doesn't normally run into people whom you can immediately identify as a great force of history. They usually reside in books, or sometimes, like Daumier Carini, in movies. One can read about and imagine the enthusiasm of the modernist ideologues who built the French Grand Ensemble, but that is not the same as sitting down with them for a chat.

Just the other day I did encounter a genuine force-of-history guy, an incarnation of the real people who lurk behind all the Ruptured Cities sprinkled through this book. He came walking right into our office and set up a presentation in our conference room. He looked entirely nondescript and nonthreatening: not young, not old; not stout, not slim; not well dressed, but not shabby; just a guy, maybe a "*banality of evil*" guy.

Actually, he is a sales rep for a prefabrication company that the San Francisco Mayor's Office of Housing wants us to consider for a homeless veterans project we were just starting to design. In fact, we may have no choice. Faced with the overwhelming need to house the homeless, the Mayor's Office, sponsor of many of our projects, is flirting with prefabrication as a means of increasing production and containing runaway cost. The same old arguments for factory-produced housing that have been around since 1946 have been revived.

Remember that adaptations of the WWII production methods that made Liberty ships and B-24s by the zillions were supposed to be the answer to the postwar housing crises. For fundamental reasons, some too wonky to burden this book, that never happened. But the big reason is that the inherently erratic and cyclical housing market is a far better match to the instantly mobilized and demobilized stick-building industry than it is to a capital-intensive factory system that must keep producing regardless of demand, incurring staggering storage costs and space utilization issues. You can't keep a neighborhood waiting in storage until a complicated multiparty, mixed-finance, and municipal entitlement deal comes together.

The seventy-year battle between factory-made housing and site-fabricated housing has some things in common with the US Air Force's failed campaign against the North Vietnamese highway system. The destruction wrought by an entire squadron of B-52s flying long range could be repaired overnight by a bunch of industrious, low-skill people with picks and shovels. Capital-intensive vs. labor intensive (except it also took lots of very expensive labor to fly and maintain the B-52s).

The sales rep explained all the oft-claimed advantages of cost and time that accrue when people are housed in rows and rows of stacks and stacks of factory-produced identical boxes, each with a rudimentary breathing hole punched in one side. Of course, he explained, it is possible (at considerable additional cost) to add some lumps and bumps on the outside of the stacked boxes, to (sort of) disguise what they are. And it is possible to make buildings that are mostly rows of stacked boxes, and partially something else, but that is far less efficient than having the prefabricators do the whole thing.

It is not as if making identical boxes in a factory and then stacking them up in rows is a big new idea. It is a variation on exactly the same idea, with exactly the same forcefully stated rationale, (*logique de grue*) that produced the catastrophic Grand Ensemble; the same idea that produced the vast areas of ghastly housing all over Eastern Europe; the same idea and rationale behind the cultural disaster of the last few hundred million units of housing in China. How is it that not only these manufacturers who stand to profit, but idealistic young architects in our own office, eager to be at the forefront of technology, buy into these ancient claims and don't see the implications?

Tectonics

I have often regretted that the kinds of buildings we usually get to design are entrapped by reasons of cost in a flimsy and primitive building technology of wood frame or light metal frame structure, wrapped mostly in cheap cladding of synthetic materials such as elastomeric stucco or cementitious siding. Ticky-tacky.

I long for and admire buildings such as those of Michael Hopkins or Todd Williams and Billie Tsien, influenced by Louis Kahn, or those of the Roman rationalists, made from steel, concrete, or structural masonry—with beautiful details, expressive of how they were made, enduring, timeless, real. No veneers; nothing fake. A few times in fifty years I have had the chance to build this way. Each time it was a joy, and I am good at it despite not much practice.

Meanwhile, we have made the most of ticky-tacky and have become quite good at that too. If the cost-competitive alternative to stick-framed ticky-tacky is stacks of prefabricated boxes, I want to rise to the defense of tick-tacky and make some claims for what we have been able to do with it. The beauty of stick framing is that it has no inherent beauty and very little inherent logic. You can bend it, twist it, make it lumpy, make it smooth, and there is no God of Tectonics to say no. The nontectonics of stick framing has enabled us to do something important. We have created a delicately nuanced architecture of place, using the flexibility of the "system," if one can call it that, to calibrate our buildings to the microcontexts they are part of, not as passive camouflage, but as part of an ethos of belonging. For low-income people, for students, for immigrants—for everyone really, belonging is a big deal, the Heideggerian big deal described in chapter 14, "Three Giants and a Midget." The nontectonics of stick framing has allowed us to find a sense of mission, and (I like to think) has made some beautiful buildings.

This does not mean we should not use the force-of-history prefabrication system if we are pressured to do so. To be an architect at all, one must be pragmatic about the march of technology and find some accommodation. One of the most intelligent pieces of work we have ever done is the extremely efficient, rational system we developed for Binhai, satisfying the demands of the technocrats but sustaining our own agenda for a rich, complex urban place. We are clever people, and perhaps we can use this prefabrication system without succumbing to it, perhaps making enough of our building site-built. But to succeed in this tricky endeavor, we must see the system as the baleful, homogenizing force it is.

The Love versus Hope idea pits soulfulness—myth, history, memory, love of place, the hopelessly subjective—against the tyranny of scientific rationalism. This argument is restating the lament of giants from Oswald Spengler to Lewis Mumford and onward. This great lineage of thinkers does not argue against science and rationalism per se, but against the passive, uncritical acceptance of its product, and against the denial of every aspect of the human that does not fit empirical measure.

CHAPTER 17

CNU: The Thirty-Year War— New Urbanism and the Academy

In the early 1990s I helped found the Congress for the New Urbanism and to write its charter, advocating the principles the Continuous City. In the ensuing twenty-five years the CNU has had an impact, mostly positive, on development practice and planning law in much of the United States. Organizations like the American Planning Association and the Urban Land Institute have adopted the language and ideas of the CNU Charter as their own—compact, walkable, transit served, mixed-use, mixed-income neighborhoods honoring local building traditions, climate, and culture. Amid this modest success there is a conspicuous failure—the widespread disdain for New Urbanism among architects, particularly the faculties of most architecture schools.

To most American architects and almost all schools of architecture, New Urbanism is a bizarre, little-known subculture that they look upon with attitudes that range from indifference to dismissiveness to active hostility. Many in CNU happily return the favor and see the digital razzle-dazzle and sheer goofiness that plasters the walls of most schools of architecture not only as meaningless, but as a virulent menace to urban civilization, poisoning the minds of the young.

This is neither a new story nor a big mystery. New Urbanists look back at certain moments of urban history with admiration and longing that is hard not to call nostalgia, and for many New Urbanists that enthusiasm extends to the architecture of olden times. For people trained and acculturated in the normal ways of architects, looking back to look forward is an apostasy against the very bedrock of a belief system rooted in modernism as perpetual revolution. For them, the CNU is Lot's wife incarnate.

One can expend a great deal of philosophical hot air on what comes down to affinities for old-fashioned versus new-fangled and not really get anywhere.

It is much too easy to say, as many CNUers have for a long time, that *they*, that phalanx of others marching with linked arms, are simply wrong in their fetishizing of autonomous object buildings at the expense of the city, and perverted in their promiscuous embrace of formal invention, the weirder the better.

I have a question to direct at those hard-core New Urbanist cadres. What if those linked-arm architects and educators goose-stepping to the drumbeat of eternal novelty are right? What if they are even a little right and New Urbanists are a little wrong? Is there something New Urbanists have been missing all these years that has helped relegate them to the far suburbs of architectural discourse? Just because people act crazy does not mean they are wrong, or always wrong.

The vast distance between what architects are taught to think is important and what New Urbanists think is important has survived radical climate change in the universities where architecture schools reside. The changes are huge. Remember Cartesian rationalism and logical positivism? Do you remember when social science dressed as science; when psychology was behaviorism; when, for a while, statistics (at least at Berkeley) was as basic to the architectural curriculum as statics, because architecture was social science plus engineering; and engineering was not today's Calatrava-vavavoom stuff; beams and columns were shaped like moment diagrams—the right way, and they'd better show.

Unfortunately, rational Cartesian solids scattered on the tabula rasa of the graph-paper city were not a big hit. Other stuff came along: Vincent Scully, Robert Venturi's *Complexity and Contradiction in Architecture*, Heideggerian voodoo, Gaston Bachelard's *The Psychoanalysis of Fire*, then weirder stuff of all sorts.

Architecture was in the bus with the rest of the university on the great journey from modernism to postmodernism. From absolutism to absolute relativism; from certainty about certainty to disbelief in belief. Architectural academics went on the long bus ride with all their academic brethren with hardly a sideways glance at the city out the window. The bus drivers came from the English department or else they were French. There were a few unruly passengers like Berkeley philosopher John Searle who said, memorably, that bus driver Jacques Derrida was the sort of person who gave bullshit a bad name, but mostly the passengers were well behaved on the ride, happily singing "100 Bottles of Beer on the Wall," although many of us had no idea where the bus was headed or why, or even what the bus drivers were all about.

One thing didn't change in the new landscape. Object fetishism, the city be damned, is the common core shared by old-style modernist Cartesian rationalism and the postmodern architecture of personal narrative. It is what links the exquisitely detailed steel boxes of yore to the blobs and the shards of today: two kinds of rigor that both face solipsistically inward. As it turned out, the preoccupation with the idealized objecthood of modern architecture has outlasted the long-spent ideas and attitudes that once gave modern architecture its moral and intellectual force and legitimacy.

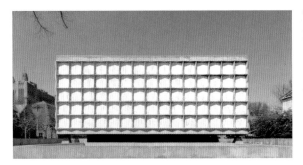

Beinecke Library, Yale; Gordon Bunshaft, 1963

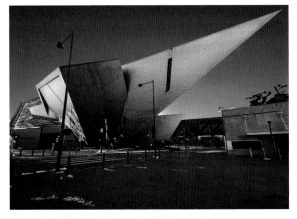

Denver Art Museum, Daniel Libeskind, 2006
Photo ©Austin Matherne

The (so far) unbreachable chasm between New Urbanism and what now passes for architectural culture consists of opposite conceptions of the relationships of place, time, and objects—not small matters. For architects, the culture of objects, their history, and the discipline of making them are infinitely rich subjects. For urbanists, objects, especially buildings, have meaning only as the constituent elements of places. This is not just a matter of—*I'm more interested in this and you're more interested in that*—like, say, botany and astronomy. Botanists and astronomers have nothing against one another—unless they happen to be competing for faculty FTE or parking. By contrast, there is real animus between the object people and the place people. Each subject has its own historiography—one focused on canonical buildings, the other on the history of the city. They not only see each other as a threat to what they hold most dear; they regard each other as uncouth, uncultured philistines.

One purpose of this book is to probe for a way out of this apparently hopeless impasse. It requires a healthy dose of the self-critical among my New Urbanist friends and sympathy for the claim that as CNU has evolved—perhaps devolved—over twenty-five years, it has narrowed and ossified into a sometimes dreary orthodoxy that betrays the subtlety, complexity, and richness of its original premise.

There was a stern warning of early-onset ossification a long time ago that went largely unheeded. It was delivered with the full might of Churchillian rhetorical flourish by New Urbanism's most formidable godfather, Colin Rowe, in a small conference at Seaside, Florida, a few weeks before his death in 1999. I wrote a chapter in *Global City Blues* about this event, but I have been thinking more about its significance recently.

Most people at that memorable conference attributed Colin Rowe's cruelty to our most esteemed colleagues to the misery of a dying man, or perhaps to the joyous freedom he felt to be released at last from the bondage of civility. What he really felt, I believe, was a sense of betrayal as he looked at some of the latest work of CNU's leaders. He saw his own influence oversimplified and trivialized, and he was deeply troubled.

The whole thrust of his Cornell Urban Design Studio, of most of his own writing, and the work and writing of the people he most influenced, is the endlessly interesting, eternally complex mediations between architecture and the city, and between history and the imperatives of an ever-changing present. He considered these mediations one of the highest manifestations of human intelligence, and never a simple matter reducible to formulae and standard practices.

To make sense of Rowe's reflexive hostility to much of what he saw at Seaside that day, I will cite two buildings and a book. The point of these three examples is that they represent the dialectic or *pas de deux* of architecture and the city at its best moments. Rowe was fond of the phrase "healthy intercourse" to describe these interactions, and he had in mind something more complex, varied, and interesting than the basic missionary position.

New Urbanism does provide a place, but a limited and condescending place, for the object obsessions and formal preoccupations of architects. It is the idea of fabric and monument. In this conception, the normative buildings of the city are an anonymous tapestry that defines and frames a few special sites for buildings of special importance—the monuments.

This conception of fabric and monument has a pedigree that includes the writings of Leon Krier and Aldo Rossi, and their precursors. It is embedded in the Charter for the New Urbanism and it is as far as most New Urbanists have considered the subject. New Urbanists (Andres Duany is one) often point to Frank Gehry's iconic Guggenheim Museum in Bilbao, and its relationship to the historic fabric that frames it, as an example of how welcoming a New Urbanist conception of the city is to eccentric and monumental modern architecture.

I want to argue (blasphemously) that the fabric/monument conceit is simplistic, condescending to architects, and not a very useful model for the various interactions between architecture and city form. A big problem with the New Urbanist fabric/monument idea is the attitude toward city fabric as something normative, ordinary, and requiring a lesser architectural intelligence than the creation of monuments—a cake mix theory of the city: take a figure/ground with continuous street walls, just add biofiltered storm water, and mix—*et voilà*: New Urbanism. In fact, as Colin Rowe knew well, the reconciliation of complex building programs with the spatial demands of the

Bilbao Guggenheim, Frank Gehry

city and the shaping of its public spaces is an architectural task of the highest order.

As the New Urbanist story goes, exceptional programs deserve exceptional sites, and jazzy buildings like the Bilbao Guggenheim belong dotted around the city, terminating axes, occupying honorific park sites, and so on. The city is not that simple, however, and not that static. Only now and then will there be congruence between isolated honorific sites and important building programs. Very often, important buildings occupy ordinary sites, and ordinary buildings occupy important sites. In a city master-planned and vigilantly administered by God, that might not be true, but so far God has received no such commission, thank God. The city is complex and messy, always changing, never divine, always pragmatic, always human. The highest calling for an architect should be to master the complex and the messy, to summon all of his skills to resolve with elegance the contradictory demands placed upon him. Mastery of the contradictory is the measure of humanity.

Consider what happens when the messy and the complex take the form of a special and important building program, like a museum or church, landing on an ordinary site, a typical lot embedded in the city fabric. Such a circumstance is not an anomaly or a mistake. Given the normal dynamics of institutions and real-estate transactions, it is bound to happen with great frequency. An architect has ample room for failure with a commission like this. If the work is too deferential to the city context, it buries the special building in its fabric and fails to give the special building the symbolic importance and recognition it needs. If the work is so eccentric that it disrupts the city fabric, it brings discredit on the institution it is attempting to honor, because eccentric buildings on ordinary sites look silly. Like someone in party dress in the daily workplace.

There is, however, a whole category of masterworks that one can call *Buildings of the Third Kind*. In these works, architects give expression and honor to special places, while simultaneously reinforcing the weave of city fabric that defines its streets and public places. Rome, with its thousands of churches, palazzos, and institutions woven through the city, has scores of *Buildings of the Third Kind*, none more masterful that those of Francesco Borromini. Borromini was eclipsed for much of his career by the flashier and more charismatic Gian Lorenzo Bernini, and his oeuvre are mostly second-tier commissions—smallish buildings on undistinguished city sites. His greatness is built on surmounting the contradictory demands of these commissions —simultaneous city fabric and monument. Second-tier commissions produced some of the most complex and subtle works of the Western canon: San Carlo alle Quattro Fontane, Sant'Ivo, Collegio Pamphili.

San Carlo alle Quattro Fontane, Francesco Borromini, Rome

Never have the ordinary and the extraordinary been reconciled with more sublime elegance than at San Carlo alle Quattro Fontane. Its interior is nothing less than a three-dimensional cosmological map, depicting in its intricate geometries and its filtration of light the relationship of heaven and Earth. But the sanctuary of San Carlino sits on an unremarkable street corner on the consistent street frontage of via Quirinale, leading to the magnificence of Palazzo Quirinale and Piazza Quirinale a couple of blocks up the street. Mediating between the glories of the interior and the important but subservient role of the exterior is a subtly undulating wall, true to the demands of both inside and out. In this most complex of mediations, Borromini leaves the enduring lesson of how to be both a humble city builder and an architect of thundering power.

Less remotely in time and place, San Francisco's great neoclassicist of the early twentieth century, Arthur Brown Jr., managed a similar feat with his monumental synagogue, Temple Emanu-El. The program is larger and more complicated than San Carlino, but it too is on an ordinary corner site with a sanctuary, a courtyard, and many more ancillary spaces than Borromini had to contend with. Brown's sanctuary is a divine geometric construct based on the domes of Sinan in Istanbul. The dome is a monumental civic presence in the city skyline. The ancillary functions are shaped into a respectful street wall, pierced on one side by a noble arch and monumental stair, and on the other by a transparent arcade, both leading to a beautiful forecourt and entry to the sanctuary.

The most clear and systematic explication of Colin Rowe's conception of architecture and the city in healthy intercourse is Michael Dennis's great book *Court and Garden*,[1] which should be required reading for all who lay claim to being New Urbanists and absolutely mandatory for students of architecture. It is tragic that this great didactic text is mostly a dust collector in university libraries these days. Dennis's book lays bare the secrets of generations of Parisian architects who brought about the most virtuosic mediations between the traditional city as the grand setting for civic life and the emerging complexity of building programs with specialized internal demands. The French Hotel, or large private aristocratic house, and its shaping of the splendors of Paris's public realm from the seventeenth to the nineteenth centuries, is a textbook for the modern city.

Rowe had only one opportunity for a comprehensive review of New Urbanists' work at Seaside. He thought his legacy was debased by what he saw as simplistic and cartoonish. Figures and grounds, fabrics and monuments—okay for a start, but not what he had devoted his life to. He found them as inadequate, as strangling of aspiration, as with all other reductive formulae. Whatever happened to Borromini and Arthur Brown, to buildings of the third kind, and to the beautiful fabric of Paris?

Temple Emanu-El, Arthur Brown Jr., San Francisco

CHAPTER 18
Mêtis

"From the arrogance that thinks it knows all truth, O God of truth, deliver us."[1]

—MISHKAN T'FILAH

Most of us have had experience with good doctors and bad doctors. The classification of knowledge into ever-finer categories has given us orthopedists, surgeons, and gastroenterologists who are whiz kids in their field, or tiny segments of it, but have neither knowledge nor curiosity about much else. When what ails you crosses the boundaries of their specialized certitude they are helpless, hopeless, not qualified, and usually not interested. You can tell by the look in their eyes.

The best doctors are different and not so common. They are the ones who defy and transcend the classifications in their medical school curriculum that divide the body into discrete systems, and most of medical practice into discrete specialties. Every once in a while, if you are lucky, you can find a doctor who escaped the classification trap and is capable of looking in an informed way at an entire human being. Doctors who do this are brave and rare, because to grapple with the complex mind/body, multisystem interactions of a whole person, they must step out of the entire epistemological structure of peer-reviewed, empirically verified and replicable certainty, into another realm of knowledge that involves speculation, feel for the subject, focus on the uniqueness of each patient, and lack of certitude.

City building, like medicine, has its own share of one-dimensional specialty nerds. There is a long history of urbanists resisting the mentality they attribute to engineers—from the surveyors of the nineteenth century with their mechanistic grids, to those whose life mission is expediting the flow of automobiles. The bête noir of urbanists has long been the unrepentant traffic engineer, whose unwalkable, single-purpose streets and marauding urban highways reify the stupidities of one-issue certitude. Somehow planners haven't yet been able to whip up the same froth of hostility to the traffic engineer's currently fashionable close cousin, the hydrologist, but the hydrologist's one-thing focus and its impact on city form is not unlike the traffic engineer. The big, swirly forms of drainage courses can be just as devastating to the tight fabric of the Continuous City as urban highways. One-issue planning is a feature of the Ruptured City, often the very cause of rupture.

In the 1990s New Urbanism was launched as reaction to the hegemony of one-dimensional one-thingers. The passion that launched New Urbanism was love of cities in all their unfathomable complexity, and revulsion at the entrenched set of simplistic conventions that produced the inverse of urbanism—amorphous, nonurban sprawl. New Urbanists aspired to be holistic, big-picture good doctors for the city. Zoning by segregated land use and the divine right of traffic engineers were the immediate first targets.

New Urbanism did not set out (originally) to provide a codified universal template for all human habitat. Certainly it did not intend to be a stylistic straitjacket imposing architectural right-think, but some strange things have happened along the way.

Like other powerful ideas, New Urbanism lingered and spread, and it has reappeared under other names like "smart growth" and "sustainable urbanism." And like other powerful ideas, it has mutated as it has metastasized and gotten weird in multiple ways. Like other assaults on orthodoxy, it has become an orthodoxy (or several), with all the attendant apparatus—its own competing saints and votaries, its own Holy See.

New Urbanism started out on the right track—challenging "I know one thing" certitude with a more complex and nuanced vision of the city. But recently it has switched to parallel tracks that lead to their own dead ends, to other forms of sterile Cartesian certitude. New Urbanists have set out to replace narrow, reductive certainty with broad, all-embracing, reductive certainty. Instead of the "I know one thing" certitude of the orthopedist or traffic engineer, there is the quest for "I have a system that explains everything, and everything I can't explain is crap" certitude. The Smart Code, initiated by Andres Duany with a legion of collaborators, is an attempt to provide prescription for almost everything, everywhere. The ambitions of LEED-ND are only slightly more modest.

The search for universal systems that explain and prescribe everything is by no means restricted to urbanists, new or old. All-embracing cosmologies are a common human quest with a long history. Christopher Alexander's *On the Nature of Order* is one such endeavor. Thomas Aquinas, Sigmund Freud, and Karl Marx are among those who also had a go at it, with mixed results.

The superb book *Seeing Like a State* [2] by Yale anthropologist and historian James C. Scott engages in a multifront combat with this long history of grand systems of description and prescription. It has the telling subtitle *How Certain Schemes to Improve the Human Condition Have Failed*. This book is not simply a history of the failure of grandiose all-embracing systems; it is a tract on the epistemology of the failure of grandiose systems—why failure is inherent in their very conception.

Scott builds his argument through a series of case studies:

— Stalinist collective farms

— Tanzanian planned agricultural villages

— A variety of other instances of simplifying and rationalizing local agriculture sponsored by the International Monetary Fund

— The building of Brasilia

He makes the case that each of these high-modernist abstract, utopian schemes was inherently blind to the particularities and nuances of local context and therefore was doomed to utter disaster economically, culturally, and ecologically. The complex ecology of the Continuous City, with its interacting spatial, temporal, and social dimensions, is not susceptible to reductive systematizing.

Of the grandiose systems that Scott chronicles, only Brasilia is explicitly about city building. Brasilia is the federal capital of Brazil, designed by urban planner Lucio Costa and architect Oscar Niemeyer, built ex nihilo starting in 1956 and opened for business in 1960. Brasilia is the largest and purest realization of the Radiant City as it was imagined by Le Corbusier in the 1920s, codified in his Athens Charter of 1943, and peddled around the world in the years before and after WWII by the Congress Internationale de la Architecture Moderne (CIAM), of which Costa and Niemeyer were founding members.

The most famous images of Brasilia show Oscar Niemeyer's monumental public buildings, great swoopy things reminiscent of General Motors styling of the same era, set in vast open spaces. There were also big, anonymous office blocks for the various ministries, and some distance away, rows of residential superquadrats, all practically self-contained, and each possessing its own commercial and leisure centers, green spaces, schools, churches, etc.

Its creators intended that every element, from the layout of the residential and administrative districts (often compared to the shape of a bird in flight) to the symmetry of the buildings themselves, should be in harmony with the city's overall design.[3]

—FROM THE UNESCO WORLD HERITAGE SITE

Superquadrat, Brasilia

Scott claims that as this Radiant City came to be, the main thing it radiated was the raging hostility of its new residents to life in the superquadrats. Not until the explosion of Chinese urbanization thirty years later was the life of a town forced into the shape of an idealized abstract diagram on such a large scale. Forced and enforced, as the Brazilian federal government has considered the purity of the Costa plan to be a symbol of national pride and has resisted any change to the original core of the city. The UNESCO website acknowledges:

. . . pressures exerted on the heritage site include real estate development, the illegal occupation of public areas and green spaces, the implementation of activities inconsistent with the end use of particular sectors, the encroachment of private property on the lakefront, increased urban traffic, and inadequate public transportation associated with social-spatial segregation across the metropolitan region.

A construction enterprise of this scale required an army of construction workers, who were housed in a spontaneous settlement of their own making. This teeming instant favela was dense, messy, and lively—as different as one could possibly imagine from the giant bars of sanitized midrise superblocks of the new capital.

Scott argues that the original Brasilia was unsustainably alienating, that the city could never have grown to 2.8 million souls but for the existence of the old favela, which has expanded, become permanent, and is where the real life of the town takes place. The utopian plan is actually sustained by the ad hoc organic community it was intended to replace—the Ruptured City sustained by the Continuous City.

The philosophical problems that Scott finds in Brasilia and his other case studies apply with equal force to the attempts to turn New Urbanism into universal codes that will get everything right—the Smart Code, LEED-ND, and their brethren. His argument also applies to the tactically useful, but inherently reductive and dreary, attempts to justify urbanity with unassailable "metrics." Winston Churchill described the hated arithmetic lessons of his childhood as "descent into the dismal bog of sums."[4] So it is with us. We can make great use of knowing how much CO_2 per capita is generated in Manhattan versus Atlanta, but one cannot even begin to understand or communicate the magic of New York that way. George Gershwin and Woody Allen have found better ways.

The universalizing codes and the metrics fetish are the displacement of what ancient Greeks called mêtis knowledge, which is always a contextual and particularized feel for a subject. The displacement is caused by the seductiveness of two other kinds of ancient Greek knowledge. They are têchnê and epistêmê, abstract universal technical knowledge and abstract reasoning. In each of Scott's case studies, grand modernist schemes based on têchnê and epistêmic knowledge displaced or attempted to displace successfully functioning systems based on mêtis. The results were catastrophic in each case except Brasilia, where epistêmê is actually sustained by mêtis.

The doctor who has the intuition to suspect that a neurological problem just might be related to nutrition, or stress, or the body instinctively protecting an old injury is practicing mêtis. Most doctors, especially those with advanced specialty training, won't rely on or cultivate their capacity for mêtis. And urbanists with a hyperfocus on empirically verifiable metrics or on universally applicable systems are doing very much the same thing. In architecture and urbanism, the impulse to displace mêtis with têchnê and epistêmê was famously labeled "physics envy" by Dennis Scott Brown years ago.

Some of our friends in philosophy departments like to think that the history of ideas precedes and shapes the history of events. Well, maybe yes, sometimes a little. The road from John Locke to Jefferson and Hamilton is pretty direct, but the winding path from Nietzsche to Mussolini is much less clearly marked. So it is with city building. One cannot expect people immersed in the complicated hurly-burly of building things to have their intellectual history straight or their acts consonant with a school of thought. Still, one can associate ways of building with ways of thinking; also, thinking about thinking can help us understand ways of building. Mêtis and the complex, unsystematic City of Love that evolved over time are a compatible pairing; one does not cause the other, but they get along; they are a happy couple.

Grand, overreaching systems also have inherent practical, economic, and political problems when it comes to city building. The ever more complicated bureaucratization of virtue á la LEED-ND or the Smart Code is not a small problem.

When urbanism is reduced to bureaucratic standards, urbanists join the disability zealots, storm-water enthusiasts, native plant eugenicists, fire-safety martinets, traffic engineers—all the legions of advocates for good causes who have codified their beliefs into the strangling miasma of conflicting hyperregulation that devours the days of those who build, and sucks life out of the American economy. The codification of the dimensions of urinals in six conflicting codes with overlapping jurisdictions is a problem. The codification of every dimension of a city design is a vastly bigger problem. This poison bathwater jeopardizes babies at the hands of an ever-growing libertarian mob that sees planning of any sort, urbanism of any sort, as part of the impedimentary crap that must be thrown out for America to become American.

So in addition to being a philosophical impossibility, it is political and economic suicide for urbanism in a time when every institution and segment of society that needs physical shelter wants to find it on the cheap. There could be no greater boost to the forces of sprawl, urban rupture, and environmental degradation than for urbanism to require the enfranchisement of a vast consultant class to hack through a self-created jungle of hyperregulation.

But there is a more interesting and hopeful side to the story. Let's go back to *Seeing Like a State*.

Scott contrasts New Urbanism's arch heroine, Jane Jacobs, with its Antichrist, Le Corbusier. Jacobs is the apostle of mêtis and Le Corbusier's city planning is the embodiment of Cartesian têchnê and epistêmê. Scott comes to the same conclusion that many others have: that Jane Jacobs's writings represent the truth of human experience, and that Le Corbusier was a pernicious madman who brought great harm to the world.

My own view is that Scott, like many others, does not fully understand Le Corbusier or what his seductive power consisted of. There is a difference, a profound and fundamental difference, between Le Corbusier and the generations of his acolytes who rebuilt much of the world so badly in his name.

On one hand, there is Le Corbusier the dogmatic utopian of the Athens Charter, Brasilia's birth parent. On the other hand, there was Le Corbusier the very fine artist, the zany cutup, the wit, the libertine, the stylish dandy who accompanied Josephine Baker from Brazil, the reverent student of Mediterranean culture, the dazzling architect of exquisitely complex buildings. None of that is captured in the ninety-five little prescriptions of the Athens Charter.

My generation and the ones before and after me swallowed the Athens Charter, only because of everything else Le Corbusier was. How could someone so brilliant and amusing, someone who made such beautiful things, be wrong about the shape of the city? One wonders what Le Corbusier's influence would have been if he had had the wisdom and the cool of Socrates, who refused to write anything down and thereby transform the nuanced contextualism of his conversations into a set of codified rules. Would Corbusian dialogue, like Socratic dialogues, have captured his other sides and produced a better world than the Athens Charter?

There is a difference between the contradictory complexity of Le Corbusier himself and the reductive simplicity of most Corbusians, as there are similar differences between Freud and most Freudians, between Marx and most Marxists, and, as Andres Duany has argued in his *Heterodoxia Architectonica*, between Palladio and most Palladians.

Duany loves to provoke, and *Heterodoxia Architectonica* is a provocation to the chummy orthodoxies of classical architecture enthusiasts, including the Institute for Classical Architecture and most of the Notre Dame architecture faculty. They are a kind of club of cultivated souls who long achingly for a world as portrayed in the early episodes of *Downton Abbey*, before WWI and its attendant nastiness. Duany's thesis is that Palladio's *Four Books on Architecture*, the basis of Thomas Jefferson's architecture and the entire international Palladian tradition, was actually a superficial tourist's view of Rome and misrepresented the nuanced complexity and inventiveness of Roman architecture. *Heterodoxia* chronicles a living heritage of particularized, contextual architectural invention from republican Rome onward.

Duany, it seems, is simultaneously a systematizer of the grandest and most reductive sort, and a subtle, nuanced idiosyncratist (if that is a word); simultaneously an ideologue and devastating debunker of orthodoxies. There is some deep, internal war between the brain hemispheres going on in the person who could produce as interesting and original a work as *Heterodoxia*, while dreaming about the simplistic utopia of the Smart Code at the same time.

Sometime after Hurricane Katrina, Duany wrote a particularly beautiful and insightful observation of New Orleans. He said that the culture of New Orleans was based on the fact that people of very modest means, mostly African American and Cajun, had title to their houses and no debt. Families lived in communities, modestly but comfortably, without the constant pressure of mortgage payments. People did not have to work frantically to subsist. That left time for the cuisine of slow-cooking stews, the culture of the church, and for a music of great complexity and richness to evolve. If urbanists care about sustainability, the sustaining of urban culture should be the first order of business. The way they cook stews and make music in New Orleans; the way they dance in Havana, dress in Milano, use language in London, look cool in Tokyo, wisecrack in New York. Those are things for us to care about.

Perhaps the most brilliant and eternally entertaining debunker of pretentious, overreaching systems of thought is Vladimir Nabokov. Over and over through his novels and critical essays, he casts the great systematizer, Sigmund Freud, as his favored whipping boy. As one whose entire world was twice totally ruptured by grand systems—first by the Bolsheviks and second by the Nazis, Nabokov had visceral distaste for what he called "the social-scene commentators, the moralists, the idea mongers."[5]

For Nabokov, idea mongering stands in the way of perception, especially perception of the most subtle and beautiful things. His Freudians, with their little system of prefabricated categories for people, are the ones who know nothing of butterflies or orchids, cannot converse with children, and don't understand the rapture of an acrobat. When asked what the color red symbolizes in *Lolita*, Nabokov replied that he

> *finds the use of symbols hateful because it substitutes a dead general idea for live specific impression. The shades of, or rather colors of say, a fox, a ruby, a carrot, a pink rose, a dark cherry, a flushed cheek, are as different as blue is from green.*[6]

In other words, it is the particular, the nuanced, and the contextual that have meaning, not the general, categorical, or abstract. Cities and parts of cities are foxes, rubies, and carrots, not "red"; mêtis is the special intelligence of great city builders.

CHAPTER 19
Place and the Displaced

"Patronizing rationality is a pervasive modern form of violence."[1]

—PETER BUCHANAN, THE BIG RETHINK

Mediterranean refugees, 2016

There are big reasons to tell the stories of the City of Love and the City of Hope; reasons these stories should be disentangled from the political and architectural histories in which they have been embedded and obscured. As this is written, the number of displaced people worldwide in need of shelter stands at 65.6 million. The number of chronically homeless in the United States is approximately 650,000. These hideous numbers do not represent a temporary problem, or an anomalous spike that will somehow abate any time soon. The large-scale migrations of people from one cultural setting to another will go on and on, and there is a permanent underclass left behind by technology and the formation of wealth. These are structural conditions of our

Century 21, with roots as deep as the inequities of capitalism, ecological change and global warming, religious and ethnic conflicts measured in millennia, automation and the march of technology—big inexorable facts about our century and our world.

As this is written, there is a political wind from Australia to Austria with the US squarely in the middle that will make matters worse, at least for a while. It is a political wind that victimizes the victims of displacement, despises them for their helplessness, and fears them for their otherness. But it is the nature of political winds to shift; eventually they always do and cycles of compassion overtake cycles of xenophobia and bigotry. Sometimes it has taken decades, warfare, and millions of deaths for the shift to occur; sometimes shifts are rapid and peaceful. We can hope and press for the latter and prepare ourselves.

So far, however, our preparations for a next age of compassionate city building are terrible. We not only have not learned the lessons of history but have not packaged the history of housing and the city to enable a nuanced assessment of what has worked and what has failed. The Love versus Hope conceit is offered as a new lens with which to view a century of urban housing and learn its lessons.

I began to write this chapter while I was teaching at the University of Rome at a moment when the refugee nightmare was dominating the news with horrible mass drownings off the Italian coast. It was also the time when the annual meeting of an organization called the International Seminar for Urban Form (ISUF) happened to be in Rome. ISUF meetings are refereed publish-or-perish opportunities for predocs, postdocs and young faculty in planning and urban design from all over the world. I was astounded that in a jam-packed, multivenue, five-day agenda, not one of these young scholars, or the smattering of distinguished old ones who participated, had a word to say about the calamity dominating television and the newspapers. One could ask any of these colleagues what they are interested in, and they would tell you politely that humanity's biggest issue—more than sixty-five million displaced people—is not their issue.

While I encountered this academic indifference and general European confusion with the refugee crises at its doorstep, I became fascinated with the stories of Rome recounted in chapter 13. What Rome did with grace from shortly after 1870 until the early 1960s, all of Europe is unwilling to do now or has simply forgotten how.

Between and after teaching trips to Rome, I came home to San Francisco and continued to read about this Roman story of immigrants and assimilation. But back in San Francisco, I realized that every day I was walking, usually like an insensate zombie, through a massive human horror, through suffering as tragic as the vast refugee camps in Jordan or Calais that one saw almost daily on the news. San Franciscans are confronted every day with the way our society and its economy first creates and then treats human discards.

Citizens, San Francisco, 2017
Photo ©Ben Piven

I have come to believe that these two very different issues—America's displaced, and the world's displaced—both scream for the same response from us, from urbanists. The interrelated phenomena of drugs, gangs, and burgeoning homelessness in the US and the worldwide refugee crises are pieces of the same hard and complicated puzzle. In some ways it makes no sense to conflate issues that have radically different chains of causality, but in other ways they are the same issue and the relation that each has to urbanity, urbanism, urban policy, urban history, urban design, and housing design are much the same.

 While urbanists have had little or nothing to say on the matter, others have had a lot to say. There are multiple contingents in the design community who see the refugee crises as basically a huge and urgent problem in industrial design—providing shelter, lots of it, at the lowest cost and in the shortest time. It is natural that IKEA, the international embodiment of low-cost, high-design, mass-produced products, should leap into the breach with its own "solution" to the refugee housing crises, consisting of a nifty flat-packed, super-cheap little shelter—like a dog house designed by Charles Eames. Imagine hundreds of thousands of them. Imagine what kind of place that would be.

Sometimes the production of minimal shelter, mostly by the United Nations High Commission for Refugees, is accompanied by some rudimentary urban design. But the UNHCR has committed to host countries such as Jordan that refugee internment camps will not become permanent settlements. It therefore forbids the paving of streets, building sewer infrastructure, or planting a tree for shade in the 120-degree heat of the Jordan desert.

Despite all this, at places like the vast Al Za'atari camp in Jordan (now dismantled), the irrepressible need of humans to build towns asserted itself anyway. There was a main street with thriving commerce—bakeries, restaurants, service businesses of all kinds—and people did cluster their little UN living crates into a semblance of streets and courtyards.

Al Za'atari, Jordan, 2015

These days, city design and city building are never mentioned in political discourse in this country or in Europe. At the beginning of the Obama administration, *Time* magazine, and a lot of us, thought what we were getting was a New New Deal. FDR and his great advisors like Harry Hopkins had a broad vision of a remade society, in which city building, the country's infrastructure, and job creation were all parts of a coherent picture so powerful that for a time, it overwhelmed Republican opposition. In 2010 the tea party used the same words and phrases that had been used in 1932 and 1934 against the New Deal to derail Obama's helter-skelter stimulus plans that never had the force of a coherent idea. For all his reflective intelligence, Obama still doesn't seem to know what happened. Obama never understood as FDR did, and as FDR and Hopkins learned in part from Mussolini (but that is another story), the relationships among city building, the economy, housing for all, and political power. Under Hopkins, the great public works of the WPA were deliberately built with minimal use of modern technology. Their purpose and their political support were based on job creation, and certain kinds of labor-intensive inefficiency were an essential part of their strategy.

So at this writing, we have Mr. Trump with his love of gold-anodized aluminum. He doesn't seem to know or care about the other meaning of gilt that has a "u" in it, but his taste for gilded buildings, hair, faucets, and the like is at least an engagement in the physical world that none of his opponents, Left and Right, have exhibited. His own choice for secretary of HUD not only professes ignorance of the history of social housing, but active hostility to the subject he knows so little about.

But city design and the capacity of cities to assimilate the migrations of people and care for the helpless are in fact political issues—big, potent, urgent political issues. In a moment of political darkness, it is up to students of urban history to make that known. I want to put forth two propositions that come from the last hundred years of city building that address both of these human calamities.

Proposition 1 has to do with scale and the shriveled public commitment to the physical world and to taking care of the neediest people. The shriveled commitment is what we have come to expect and accept.

Consider a few numbers:

The year 1976 was not a great one for housing the poor in the United States. Very little was built, and what was built was miserable stuff—horribly planned and cheaply made of the junkiest materials. There was not even the money to maintain the terrible temporary housing stock left over from WWII that was bequeathed to public housing authorities. The HUD budget for that year was $86 billion 1976 dollars.

In 2016, HUD's total budget was $47 billion 2016 dollars. However you figure the math for fifty years of compounded inflation, the cuts to HUD are several hundred percent.

Another shocker: the federal cuts to mental health services since 1991 total $4.6 billion.

One reason that public money for housing the poor and the mentally disabled disappeared was that people, and by extension legislators, despised what had been done with public money—the instant slums of public housing and the Dickensian horrors of insane asylums. Disillusion triggered disinvestment, rather than reinvestment in new models of housing, therapy, and care. So now we have 650,000 homeless, a great many of them mentally ill, living in absolute degradation and squalor in Seattle, Los Angeles, Honolulu, Boise, and, perhaps most visibly and dramatically, San Francisco. The New Deal came about in response to the degradations of Hoovervilles, the shantytowns that sprouted up all over the country in the early 1930s. In the 2010s, we have recreated Hoovervilles all over again.

The twenty-first century as a new age of public parsimony is by no means just an American issue. Look around at what was built in the 1920s: New Amsterdam, Red Vienna, in Paris the beautiful Habitacion Bon Marché, in Rome the splendid neighborhoods for low-wage workers, in the Bronx grand housing for the Amalgamated Garment Workers.

But look at a design for refugee housing for Calais in 2016. When it comes to housing people in need, we are in the middle of whatever is the antonym of a golden age. What has happened in the last ninety years? When did sheets of raw plywood replace limestone and brick as the material of choice for low-income housing? What happened to the regimes—left, right, and center—who even in the 1930s in the midst of worldwide depression

UNHCR refugee housing, Calais, 2015

struggled mightily not to have their cities overrun with helpless crazy people, huddled in doorways.

So Proposition 1 is a very simple idea—urbanists as advocates for societal guilt with a "u"— urbanists as political warriors fighting for resources devoted to people whose own labors, station in the world, or abilities cannot pay for a decent place to live. We did it splendidly and hugely ninety years ago—why in God's name not now?

Proposition 2 is more complicated, and it is what this book is about. The history of those earlier, big twentieth-century commitments to building cities and housing the poor is really two histories. There are many examples of investments in social housing making matters worse, and many examples also of big investments in building beautifully on a large scale paying huge positive dividends over time—making cities thrive economically, relieving the sufferings of the poor, and most importantly for today—assimilating large numbers of displaced people into functioning cosmopolitan cities.

In the US, as in Europe, building in opposition to the historic patterns of cities turned isolated communities of the poor and minorities into enclaves of despair. In the US the isolated projects fed a different kind of fury. In the process of working on rebuilding public housing communities, I have come to see firsthand how the physical condition and isolation of the projects is inexorably linked to gang culture, and how gang culture supports and is supported by the drug economy. It is a common observation to anyone who spends time on any of a hundred street corners in San Francisco that the drug economy thrives on and fuels homelessness and preys on the mentally ill.

In Europe and in the US there is an indirect line of causality: city design as the agent of segregation, alienation, and violence. One wonders what will be next for the millions of people stuck for generations in the quasi-concentration camps of our day, which almost all planners and architects consider not to be their issue.

In 1996, several of us New Urbanists were invited to Harvard by Secretary Cisneros to present the ideas of New Urbanism to 400 highly skeptical public housing officials. The distinguished architect and urban designer Ray Gindroz gave a superb talk that began with one compelling image that I can neither forget nor find. It was a drawing that showed the squalid and overcrowded tenements where immigrants lived in the New York of 1900. In the street there was a horse-drawn tram, and far up the street was the emerging skyline of Midtown. Ray's point was that opportunity for the most downtrodden of the immigrant horde was visible and comprehensible—just there, just a tram ride down the street. The essential characteristic of the city as a portal of assimilation is connectedness. That idea of connection—of housing for the poor as part of the city, and of the city as a portal out of poverty—has motivated this book and all the housing and urbanism I have tried to do.

It is a great irony that the first and longest-enduring Fascist regime, despite its viciousness and brutality, left us with a brilliant model for an urbanism of assimilation What Italian cities achieved in the 1920s and early 1930s is in many ways the exact inverse of the agendas of today's worldwide wave of xenophobic wall builders.

Fascist strategy was rigid social stratification—one neighborhood for butchers, another for postmen, etc. But all these Roman neighborhoods are connected—part of the interwoven fabric of the city. Roman neighborhoods, like the HBM in Paris, like the great projects of Red Vienna, are beautiful, and beautifully built of enduring materials. They used historic models in inventive ways and were designed by the very best architects and planners. They are places of pride, most of them robustly maintained ninety years after they were built, while what little we built as housing for the poor in the US of the 1970s has fallen to pieces, along with the lives of so many of its residents.

The Love versus Hope conceit is a way of looking at this history that disentangles the intrinsic and enduring worth, and the intrinsic flaws, of these two histories from their short-lived, contingent political alliances. It is a destigmatizing strategy that enables us to learn from the achievements of regimes that history has come justly to loathe. As this is written, we are at the beginning of the Trump years, and whatever actually happens next, this is a time of dark portents. The historical cycles of dark and light are not predictable and metronomic like night and day. The tenure of political darkness is unknowable, but we can only act and think on the assumption that there will be a dawn and we should prepare.

The enduring models of egalitarian city building are models of connection, assimilation, opportunity, and hope. Much of that heritage is all through modern Rome, but there is also an American heritage of ethnic neighborhoods integrated with city fabric that have been portals of assimilation.

Hannah Arendt used the term "worldlessness" to describe the condition where a person does not belong to a place that affirms their humanity. The idea comes from Heidegger, for whom "world" could be both a noun and a verb. He spoke of "the unworlding of the world."[2] If urbanists are not world makers, who is? If the history of the great accomplishments and great failures of urbanists don't provide models for the creation of worlds for the worldless, what does?

"Place" can also be both a verb and a noun. One can place the displaced, make place for them, world them. Ninety years ago the world worlded, made worlds. Now the world has forgotten that it must; for its own survival it must, but it has almost completely forgotten how. That is our job, our biggest new job, as advocates for the making of worlds for the worldless, and as learned students and teachers of urbanism's own most noble history. There are millions of people who desperately need us to know and become advocates for our own history.

Photo ©Fred Lyon

End Notes

CHAPTER 1

1. Baldassare Castiglioni, *The Book of the Courtier* (New York: Scribners, 1903).

2. Peter Gay, *Modernism: The Lure of Heresy* (New York: Random House, 2007).

3. Aldo Rossi, *A Scientific Autobiography* (Cambridge, MA: MIT Press, 1981).

CHAPTER 2

1. H. Peter Oberlander and Eva Newbrun, *Houser: The Life and Work of Catherine Bauer* (Vancouver. BC: UBC Press, 1999).

2. Mel Scott and T. J. Kent, *New City: San Francisco Redeveloped* (San Francisco: City Planning Commission, 1948).

3. Suzanne Komossa, *Atlas of the Dutch Urban Block* (Bussum, The Netherlands: Thoth, 2005).

4. Catherine Bauer, *Modern Housing* (Boston: Houghton Mifflin, 1934).

5. H. Peter Oberlander and Newbrun Eva, *Houser: The Life and Work of Catherine Bauer* (Vancouver, BC: UBC Press, 1999).

6. Gail Radford, *Modern Housing for America* (Chicago: University of Chicago Press, 1996).

CHAPTER 4

1. Fred Lyon, *The Way It Was* (New York: Princeton Architectural Press, 2014).

2. Anne Vernez-Moudon, *Built for Change: Neighborhood Architecture in San Francisco* (Cambridge, MA: MIT Press, 1989).

3. Mel Scott and T. J. Kent, *New City: San Francisco Redeveloped* (San Francisco: City Planning Commission, 1948).

CHAPTER 6

1. Sigfried Giedion, *Space, Time and Architecture* (Cambridge, MA: Harvard University Press, 1959).

CHAPTER 7

1. Winston Churchill (www.brainyquote.com).

2. Aldo Rossi, *The Architecture of the City* (Cambridge, MA: MIT Press, 1984).

CHAPTER 10

1. Michael J Meyer, *The Last Days of Old Beijing* (New York: Walker, 2008).

2. Liangyong Wu, *Rehabilitating the Old City of Beijing* (Vancouver, BC: UBC Press, 1999).

CHAPTER 11

1. *Vers de Logements Sociaux 2* (Paris: Cité de l'Architecture & du Patrimoine, 2012).

CHAPTER 13

1. Lucio Barbera, "The Radical City of Lucovico Quaroni" (unpublished manuscript).

2. Philip V. Cannistraro and Brian R. Sullivan, *Il Duce's Other Woman* (New York: William Morrow, 1993).

3. Bruno Reichlin, "Figures of Neorealism in Italian Architecture (Part I)," Grey Room 5 (Autumn 2001): 78–101 (translated by Antony Shugaar, revised by Branden W. Joseph).

4. Lucio Barbera, "The Radical City of Lucovico Quaroni" (unpublished manuscript).

CHAPTER 14

1. Vladimir Nabokov, *Lolita* (New York: Putnam, 1958).

2. Vladimir Nabokov, *Ada* (New York: McGraw-Hill, 1959).

3. Vladimir Nabokov, *Speak Memory* (New York: Putnam, 1970).

4. Martin Heidegger, *Being and Time* (New York: Harper Perennial, 2008).

5. Charles Eisenstein, *The Ascent of Humanity* (New York: Random House, 2007).

6. Oliver Sacks, *The Man Who Mistook His Wife for a Hat* (New York: Summit Books, 1985).

CHAPTER 15

1. Sigfried Giedion, *Space, Time and Architecture* (Cambridge, MA: Harvard University Press, 1959).

2. Theodor W. Adorno, *Philosophy of Modern Music* (New York: Seabury, 1973).

3. Martin Jay, *The Dialectical Imagination* (Berkeley: University of California Press, 2008).

4. Rem Koolhaas, *Content* (Köln: Taschen, 2004).

5. www.brainyquote.com.

6. Karl Lagerfeld, "Le Style de Chanel," in *Chanel, ed. Harold Koda and Andrew Bolton* (New York: Metropolitan Museum of Art, 2005), 14–17.

7. Bernard Taper, *Balanchine* (Berkeley: University of California Press, 1987).

8. Eve Blau, *The Architecture of Red Vienna* (Cambridge, MA: MIT Press, 1999).

CHAPTER 17

1. Michael Dennis, *Court and Garden* (London: MIT Press, 1992).

CHAPTER 18

1. Mishkan T'filah (Central Conference of American Rabbis, New York, 2007).

2. James C. Scott, *Seeing Like a State* (New Haven, CT: Yale University Press, 2008).

3. whc.unesco.org.

4. www.brainyquote.com.

5. Vladimir Nabokov, *Speak Memory* (New York: Putnam, 1970).

6. Ibid.

CHAPTER 19

1. Peter Buchanen, "The Big Rethink" (*Architectural Review*, London).

2. Martin Heidegger, *Being and Time* (New York: Harper Perennial, 2008).

Image Credits

Page 38. **La Strada Novissima, 1980 Venice Architecture Biennale.** Photo from Averyreview.com.

Page 42. **San Francisco block plans.** ©John Ellis.

Page 43. **Florence Lipsky's drawing of San Francisco.** Photo from *San Francisco: The Grid Meets the Hills*. (Paris: Editions, 1999).

Page 48. **Seagram Building, Chicago, Mies van der Rohe.** Photo from Wordpress.com.

Page 48. **Pilotis Unité d'Habitation, Marseilles, Le Corbusier.** ©Chris Hellier/Alamy Stock Photo

Page 66. **Zeilenbau in its pure form.** Photo from Wordpress.com.

Page 66. Oskar **Stonorov's Carl Mackley Houses as exhibited at MoMA.** Photo from Gail Radford, *Modern Housing for America* (Chicago: University of Chicago Press, 1996).

Page 73. **Ju'er Hutong.** Photo from Sohu.com.

Page 92. **Clichy-sous-Bois, 2005.** ©Jacques Brinon / Associated Press.

Page 92. **Clichy-sous-Bois, 2005.** Photo from libcom.org.

Page 92. **Clichy-sous-Bois, 2005.** Photo from Worldpress.com.

Page 93. **Logique du Grue.** ©Mémoire2cité.

Page 96. **Cité de l'Architecture et du Patrimoine (right).** ©Hamonic + Masson & Associés.

Page 135. **South-Korea-Panama-Baseball.** ©Press Association.

Page 139. **Butterfly**. © Kenneth Dwain Harrelson.

Page 148. **Social housing, Madrid; celebrated by MoMA.** Photo from Mimoa.com.

Page 150. **Chanel classics.** Photo from Chanel by Karl Lagerfeld. ©Metropolitan Museum of Art

Page 153. **Duke Ellington.** Photo from Tumblr.com.

Page 155. **Urban infrastructure, Otto Wagner.** Photo from Abload.de.com.

Page 165. **Beinecke Library, Yale; Gordon Bunshaft, 1963.** ©Wikimedia Commons user Gunnar Klack licensed under CC BY 4.0.

Page 165. **Denver Art Museum, Daniel Libeskind, 2006.** ©Austin Matherne.

Page 168. **San Carlo alle Quattro Fontane, Francesco Borromini, Rome.** Left: Mary Ann Sullivan; middle: ©B. O'Kane.

Page 174. **Superquadrat, Brasilia.** Photo from archipostcard.blogspot.com.

Page 178. **The fox.** ©Tsaiproject on VisualHunt.com.

Page 179. **Mediterranean refugees, 2016.** Photo from rts.ch.com.

Page 181. **Citizens, San Francisco, 2017.** Photo ©Ben Piven.

About the Author

Daniel Solomon, FAIA, is an architect, urban designer, and professor emeritus whose fifty-year career combines achievements in professional practice with teaching and writing. The focus of his work has been the design of housing, much of it affordable housing, and the interaction between housing and urban design. From this base, his work has expanded to include large-scale urban planning and institutional buildings. He was one of the cofounders of the Congress for the New Urbanism and is currently a partner in the Seattle and San Francisco–based firm Mithun.

HONORS AND AWARDS

Daniel Solomon's hundred-plus design awards include the HUD Secretary's Platinum Award for Excellence on two occasions and three national honor awards from the AIA. He received the Silver SPUR Award for outstanding civic contributions in October 2013. He has twice been named one of "the 100 Foremost Architects" by *Architectural Digest* and is the 1998 recipient of the Seaside Prize for contributions to American urbanism, and the 2004 recipient of the Maybeck Award from the California AIA for achievement in design. In 2008 he was named "Housing Hero" by the Housing Action Coalition

PUBLICATION

Solomon is the author of many articles and four previous books: *ReBuilding, Global City Blues, Cosmopolis,* and an e-book, *Bedside Essays for Lovers (of Cities).* In addition to his published writing, Solomon's works have been published in most of the leading architectural journals worldwide, as well as some fifteen architectural anthologies.

TEACHING

University of California, Berkeley: Professor of Architecture, 1979–2000; Emeritus, 2000–present; Associate Professor, 1973–1979; Assistant Professor, 1967–1972; Lecturer, 1966

Visiting Professor, University of Rome, Sapienza, 2015

Visiting Professor, University of Miami, Rome, 2014

KEA Distinguished Professor, University of Maryland, 2011

Cass Gilbert Visiting Professor, University of Minnesota, 1992

Adjunct Visiting Professor, Columbia University, New York, 1987

Visiting Assistant Professor, University of Southern California, Fall 1969

Acknowledgments

I have many people to thank for all I have learned and experienced in my fifty years as an architect and teacher. The ideas and projects in this book evolved over decades, and I will not attempt to name the many friends, colleagues, students, and institutions to whom I am deeply indebted.

Just a few:

Thanks to my partners at Mithun, Seattle, and those in our San Francisco office, Mithun/Solomon, for so generously providing me personal space, time, staff support, and encouragement.

To the American Academy in Rome for the serene and stimulating environment to produce much of this book.

To Tigran Haas and Peter Elmlund, cosponsors of this book through the Centre for the Future of Places, Royal Institute of Technology, Stockholm.

To Cheryl Weber, my gentle editor.

To Kristen Bakken for joyfully designing a beautiful book.

To my encouraging critical readers: Lucio Barbera, Michael Bell, Peter Calthorpe, Jean-Francois Lejeune, Gabriel Metcalf.

To John Ellis for years of moral support, friendship, and much help with illustrations.

To Fred Lyon for capturing the soul of San Francisco.

To Jonathan Cott for nurturing the fantasy that I am a writer.

To Georgia Tech and Ellen Dunham Jones for super intern Yao Zeyue.

To Shirley for love and forbearance.

To my appropriated mentors and glorious heroes, many of whom find themselves posthumously in these pages.